UNDERSTANDING
AUTISM

An easy-to-read parenting guide
for assisting autistic families,
debunking common myths, and
celebrating autistic strengths

Diane Harvie

Table of Contents

PREFACE

Before my son's third birthday, he was diagnosed with autism. This revelation came just before Christmas 2013 and after a period of profound uncertainty and isolation, during a time when a health visitor had dismissed my concerns, suggesting they were a figment of my imagination.

For months, my world had shrunk to the confines of our home, dictated by my son's severe meltdowns. Seeking support, I reached out to my health visitor, only to be met with skepticism. I was vulnerable, grappling with the challenges of adapting to a new city without the support network of family or friends. Yet, what I encountered was a dismissal that left me feeling utterly isolated and branded as the problem — a notion that my anxiety was the root cause of my son's distress, undermining the legitimacy of his experiences and my intuition as a mother.

This accusation shattered me. Upon confiding in my husband, his outrage mirrored my own devastation. All the advice that championed seeking help now felt like a path to regret. This experience precipitated a decline in my mental well-being, leading me to seek medical help for anxiety.

Yet, less than a year later, the truth we had sensed was confirmed: our son was diagnosed as mid-spectrum autistic. This journey underscores a pervasive issue many parents face — a stigma that wrongfully assigns blame and fosters doubt. It's an injustice to feel compelled to defend your child's needs and your capability as a parent.

This book is born from a desire to offer a beacon of understanding and guidance for families navigating the complexities of autism. Recognizing that each child's journey is unique, this guide aims to offer solace and practical advice, tailored to the diverse experiences of autistic families. If it eases the path for even one family, then it has achieved its purpose.

INTRODUCTION

In the quiet of a routine evening, Sarah sat cross-legged on the living room floor. Her gaze alternated between her two-year-old son, Alex, engrossed in his world of colorful blocks and the pile of parenting books on the coffee table. None of the books seemed to explain why Alex hadn't spoken his first word, why he avoided eye contact, or why his meltdowns were so intense and frequent compared to what she read about other toddlers. It was a puzzle she felt unequipped to solve, each day ending with more questions than answers.

The journey to understanding began with a routine pediatric visit, one that shifted their world. The doctor's words, "I believe Alex may be on the autism spectrum," echoed in Sarah's mind, a blend of relief and a myriad of new fears. This moment, both isolating and defining, is one that countless parents around the globe experience each year.

Autism, a complex, multifaceted condition that affects 1 in 54 children in the United States alone, remains one of the most misunderstood aspects of child development. Despite its prevalence, the journey of raising an autistic child can feel like navigating an intricate maze without a map. Each child's unique needs and abilities can turn everyday parenting strategies into a series of trials and errors, leaving families yearning for understanding and support.

This book emerges from the heart of such stories, weaving together the shared experiences of countless families with the latest insights into autism. It aims to be the guide that Sarah, and many parents like her, search for in their quiet moments of doubt — a beacon of understanding in a journey marked by challenges and profound love.

For many parents, the journey of raising an autistic child is paved with a tapestry of complex emotions and challenges that extend beyond the child's diagnosis. The initial confusion that wraps around their hearts like a thick fog often stems from a place of love and a deep desire to understand their child's world. They grapple with questions that seem to have no immediate answers: How can I best support my child? Why does my child experience the world differently?

This confusion is compounded by the frustration of communication barriers. Conversations that seem straightforward can become intricate dances, where both parent and child struggle to find a common rhythm. The nuances of non-verbal cues, the ebbs and flows of sensory sensitivities, and the unpredictability of responses turn daily interactions into a series of painstakingly navigated exchanges.

Isolation creeps into their lives, not just in social settings where the glances of misunderstanding from others can feel like a chasm widening between them and the world, but also in private moments, where the weight of their child's needs feels like a journey they walk alone. Family gatherings become a gauntlet, fraught with the potential for judgment and misplaced advice, while the accessibility of public spaces turns into a question mark, shadowed by the unpredictability of sensory overloads.

Behavioral challenges, like navigating meltdowns that are not tantrums but a child's overwhelming response to a world that doesn't align with their sensory needs, add layers of complexity. Parents find themselves constantly advocating for their children in educational settings, fighting against a tide of misunderstanding and seeking accommodations that respect their child's unique way of experiencing the world.

Amidst these trials, societal barriers stand as formidable obstacles — misinformation, stereotypes, and the stigmatization of autism create an environment where acceptance feels conditional and the celebration of neurodiversity a distant hope. This book acknowledges these struggles not just as abstract concepts but as the lived realities of families navigating the world of autism. It's a recognition of the pain, the joy, and the profound resilience of these remarkable families.

Within these pages, you will embark on a journey that transforms uncertainty into understanding, frustration into fulfillment, and isolation into community. This book offers an insightful exploration into the autistic mind, providing you with a deeper comprehension of how your child perceives the world.

You will learn to decode the language of non-verbal communication, uncovering the nuances of what your child is expressing, even when words are scarce. Strategies for navigating daily challenges, from managing sensory sensitivities to fostering positive behaviors, will be laid out in clear, actionable steps, empowering you to create a supportive and nurturing environment for your child.

Moreover, you will gain access to practical advice on building strong, effective partnerships with educators and therapists, ensuring your child receives the understanding and support they deserve. This book doesn't just stop at coping mechanisms; it strives to celebrate the joys and strengths inherent in neurodiversity, encouraging you to see beyond the diagnosis to the unique individual your child is. By the end, you will not only feel more confident in your parenting journey but also become a fervent advocate for your child, ready to embrace and champion their place in the world.

Reading this book will serve as a pivotal turning point in your journey as a parent or caregiver of an autistic child. The first and perhaps most profound benefit is a transformative understanding of autism. By delving into the autistic mind, you will begin to see the world through your child's eyes, appreciating their unique way of interacting with their surroundings. This new perspective will not only deepen your empathy but also equip you with the knowledge to support your child's needs effectively.

Communication, often a source of frustration and misunderstanding, will become a strengthened bond between you and your child. Through practical, easy-to-implement strategies, you'll learn to navigate and bridge the gaps in communication, creating a dialogue that respects and adapts to your child's preferences. Whether your child is verbal or non-verbal, this book will enhance your ability to connect, reducing stress and increasing moments of joy and understanding.

Another key benefit is creating an autism-friendly environment. This book guides you in tailoring your home and daily routines to be more inclusive and comforting for your child, addressing sensory sensitivities and designing spaces that allow them to thrive. The emphasis on positive behavior support will offer you tools to encourage your child's development while maintaining a peaceful, nurturing home.

Beyond practical advice, this book offers emotional support, serving as a reminder that you are not alone. The shared experiences and stories within these pages will bolster your confidence and empower you with the assurance that you are doing your best. This empowerment extends to your family life, promoting a more inclusive, understanding, and supportive dynamic that celebrates your child's individuality.

Ultimately, the benefits of reading this book ripple outward, impacting not just your family but also contributing to a more accepting and informed society. By embracing the lessons and strategies offered, you'll not only advocate for your child but also pave the way for a future where neurodiversity is celebrated, not stigmatized.

My journey into the world of autism began not as an expert but as a parent, walking the same path you find yourself on today. The day my child was diagnosed, I felt a mix of emotions — fear, confusion, but most of all, a deep desire to understand and support them in the best way possible. This journey has been one of profound personal growth, filled with challenges that taught me resilience, patience, and the true meaning of empathy. Along the way, I've had the privilege of meeting countless families, each with their own unique story of love, struggle, and triumph. These encounters have enriched my understanding of autism, moving beyond the clinical definitions to the heart and soul of what it means to live a neurodiverse life.

Writing this book is my way of sharing not just what I've learned from my own experience but also the collective wisdom of the autism community. It's a reflection of the shared hopes, fears, joys, and challenges we face as parents and caregivers. My aim is not just to educate but to connect, offering a hand to hold as we navigate this journey together. This book is for you, from someone who understands deeply what it means to love and support an autistic child.

UNDERSTANDING AUTISM

CHAPTER 1

THE SPECTRUM UNVEILED

Imagine opening a box of crayons for the first time. Each color is unique, vibrant, and full of potential. This is much like stepping into the world of autism — a spectrum where each shade represents the diverse experiences and abilities of those living with autism. This chapter sets out to demystify autism, transforming it from a word that might seem complex or overwhelming into something clear, understandable, and relatable.

Autism is a broad term that covers a range of experiences, but at its core, it's about how individuals perceive the world and interact with others. Here, you won't find medical jargon or hard-to-understand concepts. Instead, you'll discover what autism means in everyday language, breaking down the barriers that often surround this condition.

You'll learn about the signs that could indicate someone is on the autism spectrum and how these signs vary widely, much like the distinct colors in a crayon box. But more importantly, you'll see the beauty and richness that autism brings to the world — challenging myths and changing perspectives.

This chapter is your starting point, guiding you through the essentials of understanding autism. It's here to provide support, offer insights, and celebrate the diversity and strengths of those on the spectrum. Welcome to a world where every color has its place and every shade is valued — a world of understanding, acceptance, and empowerment.

What is Autism? A Simplified Definition

Think of a radio, with its many stations, each playing different music, news, or talk shows. Just as you tune the radio to find a station that matches your interest, individuals on the autism spectrum tune into the world in their unique ways. Autism is a developmental condition, much like the radio, with a broad spectrum of 'stations' that represent the variety of ways autistic people communicate, behave, and interact with others.

At its core, autism affects how a person perceives the world around them and how they communicate and interact with other people. Some might find social interactions challenging, have interests that they are deeply passionate about, or experience the sensory aspects of the world — like sounds, lights, and textures — in a more intense way than others do.

However, just like every radio can tune into a multitude of stations, individuals with autism have a wide range of abilities and ways of seeing the world. No two people on the autism spectrum are exactly alike, and that's what makes the spectrum so diverse and fascinating. This spectrum includes those who might need significant support in their daily lives, as well as those who live independently, work, and have families.

In simple terms, autism is not a single condition with a one-size-fits-all description. It's a spectrum of experiences and interactions, each as unique and valuable as the next. By understanding autism as a spectrum, we can appreciate the individuality of each person's experiences and support them in the ways they find most beneficial.

Breaking Down the Jargon

In the conversation about autism, several terms frequently come up, which might seem complex at first glance. Let's simplify them:

- **Neurodiversity:** Imagine a garden with a wide variety of plants — flowers, trees, shrubs — each thriving in its own way. Neurodiversity is the idea that people's brains work in a vast range of ways, and like the plants in the garden, each has its unique beauty and contribution to the ecosystem. It celebrates the differences in how people think, learn, and interact.

- **Sensory Sensitivities**: Imagine wearing a shirt with a tag that feels like it's scratching your skin. For someone with sensory sensitivities, everyday sensations like sounds, lights, or textures can feel much more intense, sometimes overwhelming.

- **Stimming**: Have you ever tapped your pencil when thinking hard or bounced your knee while waiting? Stimming, or self-stimulatory behavior, includes movements or actions that help manage emotions or sensory input. For autistic people, it's a way to cope with stress or express joy.

Mini-Glossary:

- **Autism Spectrum**: The range of experiences and characteristics that autistic people may have.
- **Social Communication**: How we use language and non-verbal cues like gestures to interact with others.
- **Executive Functioning**: Skills for planning, focusing, and managing tasks.
- **Meltdown**: An intense response to overwhelming situations, different from a tantrum because it's not seeking attention but is a reaction to feeling overwhelmed.

Myths vs. Facts

- ✗ **Myth**: Autistic people do not want to make friends.
- ✓ **Fact**: Many autistic people desire friendships; they might just approach social interactions differently.
- ✗ **Myth**: Autism is caused by vaccines.
- ✓ **Fact**: Numerous studies have shown there is no link between vaccines and autism. Vaccines are safe and essential for health.
- ✗ **Myth**: All autistic people have an exceptional skill or "savant" ability.
- ✓ **Fact**: While some autistic individuals have remarkable talents, just like in the general population, not everyone on the spectrum has a savant ability. Each person's skills and interests are unique.

✖ **Myth**: Autism can be cured.

✔ **Fact**: Autism is a lifelong developmental difference, not an illness to be cured. The focus is on support and understanding to help autistic individuals thrive.

✖ **Myth**: Autistic people don't have emotions or empathy.

✔ **Fact**: Autistic people experience a full range of emotions and can be very empathetic. They might express their feelings differently.

The Autism Spectrum: A World of Colors

The autism spectrum is a vibrant tapestry of experiences, abilities, and ways of interacting with the world. It's not a linear path from one point to another but rather a broad, colorful spectrum — much like a rainbow that stretches across the sky after a rainstorm. Each color on this spectrum shines brightly on its own, contributing to the beauty and diversity of the whole.

Imagine the spectrum as an artist's palette, where each hue represents different characteristics, strengths, and challenges that people on the autism spectrum might have. Some individuals might resonate with the deep blues, symbolizing introspection and a rich inner world. Others might align with the bright yellows, reflecting joy in specific interests and the ability to focus intensely on what they love. Then, there are those who embody the vibrant reds, showing passion and deep emotions, sometimes too intense to contain.

This "spectral thinking" helps us move beyond the idea of categorizing people simply as 'mild' or 'severe.' It acknowledges that someone might need significant support in one area of their life while being exceptionally skilled or independent in another. For instance, a person might have difficulties with verbal communication, akin to a deep blue, yet excel in visual arts, a radiant yellow on their personal spectrum of abilities.

The autism spectrum is about recognizing and celebrating these diverse experiences. It's understanding that each person brings their unique blend of colors to the world, painting their masterpiece of life. Just as no two rainbows are ever quite the same, no two people on the autism spectrum are identical. Each individual's spectrum of colors contributes to the richness and diversity of our collective human experience, making our world a more interesting and beautiful place to live.

Profiles of the Spectrum

Within the wide expanse of the autism spectrum, there are various profiles, each with its distinct characteristics. These profiles are not steps on a ladder or rankings but rather snapshots of the diverse ways autism manifests in individuals. By sharing stories of real people, we can illuminate these profiles without placing one above another.

Ella's Story: The Detailed Observer

Ella has a deep passion for the intricacies of nature. She can name countless species of birds and their calls, a talent that amazes those around her. Ella's profile on the autism spectrum highlights her extraordinary attention to detail and ability to remember facts related to her interests. Social interactions, however, can sometimes feel like navigating a foreign country where she doesn't speak the language. Her journey illustrates a blend of remarkable skills and areas where she seeks understanding and support.

Max's Story: The Quiet Innovator

Max prefers the world of machines, gadgets, and overcrowded social gatherings. With a mind that sees in patterns and systems, he has an uncanny ability to troubleshoot and solve complex technical problems. This knack for understanding how things work makes Max an invaluable asset in his technology career. While he might find social cues and conventions puzzling, his innovative thinking showcases another facet of the autism spectrum, where unique perspectives drive creativity and progress.

Lila's Story: The Empathetic Connector

Contrary to the misconception that autistic individuals lack empathy, Lila embodies deep emotional connections with those around her. She feels the emotions of others intensely, sometimes more so than her own. Through her art, she communicates her understanding of the world and the emotions swirling within it. Lila's profile challenges stereotypes and highlights the profound empathy and creativity that can flourish on the autism spectrum.

These stories of Ella, Max, and Lila reflect just a few colors in the spectrum's vast array. Each person brings their unique blend of abilities, challenges, and perspectives, enriching the tapestry of human experience. By recognizing and celebrating these diverse profiles, we can foster a more inclusive and understanding world for everyone on the autism spectrum.

Valuing Diversity

Recognizing and valuing this diversity is not just an act of acceptance but a celebration of the myriad ways in which the human mind can perceive, interpret, and interact with the world. The strength of the autism community lies in its diversity and in the vast array of experiences, skills, and perspectives that autistic individuals bring to the table.

"Autism is not a defect but a different way of being," remarks Dr. Simon Baron-Cohen, a leading expert in autism. This perspective shifts the narrative from one of deficit to difference, acknowledging that the diversity within the autism spectrum is a form of neurodiversity that should be respected and valued.

Autistic individuals themselves speak of the importance of this recognition. "My autism is my greatest strength," says Julia, an autistic advocate. "It allows me to see the world in a unique way, to solve problems creatively, and to connect with details that others might overlook."

Valuing diversity within the autism community means moving beyond one-size-fits-all approaches to support and inclusion. It requires listening to and learning from autistic individuals about their experiences, needs, and aspirations. By doing so, we not only affirm the value of each person's unique contribution but also enrich our collective understanding of humanity.

The call to value diversity is a call to action: to create environments where all autistic individuals can thrive, to champion policies that respect and accommodate difference, and to celebrate the contributions of autistic people in all areas of life. In valuing diversity, we acknowledge the intrinsic worth of every individual and the potential for growth, innovation, and connection that lies within the autism community.

Early Signs: Knowing What to Look For

Identifying the early signs of autism can be the first step toward understanding your child's unique way of experiencing the world. While every child develops at their own pace, certain signs may indicate that a child is on the autism spectrum. These signs can vary widely, but knowing what to look for can help parents and caregivers seek the support and resources that can benefit their child's development. Here, we outline some of the early indicators of autism, organized by age and developmental stage:

From Birth to 12 Months:

- **Limited eye contact:** Your baby might not look at you as frequently as expected or might struggle to maintain eye contact.
- **Few or no big smiles:** By around six months, babies typically share big smiles or joyful expressions, especially in response to their parents. A lack of these expressions can be an early sign.

- **Little to no back-and-forth sharing:** By nine months, this includes sounds, smiles, or other facial expressions.

From 12 to 24 Months:

- **Delayed speech development:** Not using words by 16 months or phrases by 24 months is a common sign.
- **Lack of responsive gestures:** Such as pointing or waving goodbye by 12 months.
- **Less interest in social games:** Lack of interest in simple social games like 'got your nose' or 'peek-a-boo.'

From 24 Months Onwards:

- **Repetitive behaviors:** Engaging in repetitive movements, such as rocking, spinning, or flapping hands.
- **Intense interest in specific topics or objects:** Your child might focus intensely on a particular item or subject to the exclusion of others.
- **Difficulty with changes in routine:** Showing significant distress at changes in the familiar order of activities.
- **Challenges in playing or interacting with peers:** Preferring to play alone or having difficulty engaging in play that involves give-and-take with others.

Communication and Social Interaction:

- **Limited sharing of interests:** Less likely to show or bring objects to share interest or enjoyment.

- **Challenges with social reciprocity:** Difficulty in back-and-forth conversation, sharing emotions, or understanding social cues.

Behavioral Indicators:

- **Unusual responses to sensory input:** Over- or under-reacting to sensory information like textures, sounds, or lights.

- **Inflexibility with routines:** Insistence on sameness, routines, and difficulty with transitions.

It's important to remember that the presence of one or more of these signs does not definitively mean a child is on the autism spectrum. However, if you notice these signs, consider discussing them with a healthcare provider. Early intervention can significantly impact a child's development and support their growth and learning.

Parental Observations

Trusting your instincts as a parent is pivotal when it comes to understanding your child's development. Often, parents are the first to notice the early signs that may indicate their child is on the autism spectrum. It's the subtle cues, the patterns of behavior, or the missed milestones that may initially raise questions.

"I remember feeling like something was different when my son was about 18 months old," shares Maria, a mother of two. "He wasn't responding to his name and avoided eye contact. It was those little things that nudged me to seek further advice."

Similarly, David, father to a four-year-old daughter with autism, notes, "It was the way she played with her toys — lining them up meticulously and getting upset if anything was out of place. At first, we thought it was just a quirk, but it prompted us to dig deeper."

These stories underline a crucial message: parents know their children best. While not every quirk or preference signifies autism, noticing patterns that differ from typical developmental milestones can be an important first step in seeking clarification and support. Listening to your gut feeling and observing your child's interaction with their environment can guide you toward understanding their unique needs.

It's important to remember that these observations are not about labeling your child but about recognizing their individuality and ensuring they receive the support they need to thrive. Trusting your observations and seeking professional advice when necessary can make a significant difference in your child's life.

If you suspect your child might be on the autism spectrum, taking proactive steps can make a world of difference in understanding and supporting their development. Here's a practical guide to navigating this important phase:

1. **Document Observations**: Start by jotting down your observations. Note patterns, behaviors, and any developmental milestones that concern you. This record will be invaluable when discussing your child's development with professionals.

2. **Consult a pediatrician**: Your child's doctor is often the first point of contact. Share your observations and concerns openly. The pediatrician can provide initial insights and, if necessary, refer you to a specialist in developmental disorders.

3. **Seek a Specialist Evaluation**: A thorough assessment by a specialist, such as a developmental pediatrician, pediatric neurologist, or psychologist, is crucial. These professionals can conduct comprehensive evaluations to understand your child's unique profile.

4. **Explore Support Networks**: While navigating assessments, look for support networks. Connecting with other parents, autism advocacy groups, or online communities can provide valuable information and emotional support.

5. **Educate Yourself**: Learn about autism from reputable sources. Understanding the spectrum will help you advocate for your child effectively and make informed decisions about their care and support.

Remember, early intervention can significantly impact your child's development. Seeking professional guidance and tapping into support networks can provide the foundation your child needs to thrive. Your journey may have challenges, but it's filled with potential for growth and discovery.

CHAPTER 2:

MYTHS VS. REALITY

᳁

Let's clear the air. When it comes to autism, there's a thick fog of myths surrounding it. These myths? They're more than just harmless tales; they shape how we see autistic individuals, deeply affecting their lives and the lives of their families. Why is it so important to break these myths down, to shine a light on the truth? With understanding comes support, acceptance, and the right kind of help.

Autism is a spectrum, wide and varied, yet many believe in a single story. These stories, these myths, have weight. They influence how society interacts with autistic individuals, how families cope, and how autistic people see themselves. But here's the thing—myths are built on misunderstanding, not reality. By tackling these myths head-on, we're not just correcting false beliefs; we're opening doors to a world where autistic individuals are seen for who they are, not the myths surrounding them.

Let's dive into some of these myths. From the idea that all autistic people are the same to the misconception that they can't form meaningful relationships, each myth does its part in painting a picture far from the truth. With each myth debunked, we'll see autism in a new light, understanding the spectrum in its full, vibrant diversity.

But it's not just about understanding what autism isn't. It's equally about recognizing what it is. Autistic individuals possess a myriad of strengths, often overlooked because of these myths. They see the world through a unique lens, offering perspectives that can enrich our understanding, solve complex problems, and create art that moves us. Recognizing and nurturing these strengths is key to providing a foundation for autistic individuals to thrive on their own terms.

And let's not forget that autism doesn't look the same in everyone. Boys and girls, men and women, experience and express autism in ways as unique as they are. Acknowledging these differences is crucial, not only for providing the right support but for ensuring that no one is left behind simply because they don't fit a stereotype.

By stripping away the myths and embracing the reality of autism, we're not just changing perceptions; we're changing lives. With every myth debunked, every strength celebrated, and every difference acknowledged, we move closer to a world where autistic individuals are valued for who they are, not defined by misconceptions. This chapter is more than just words on a page; it's a step toward understanding, acceptance, and support for all autistic individuals. Let's embark on this eye-opening journey together, leaving myths behind and embracing the beautiful reality of autism.

Debunking Common Autism Myths

Where do these myths about autism come from? Often, they're born from incomplete information, outdated beliefs, or even popular media's simplified portrayals. These myths aren't just harmless misunderstandings; they carry weight. They shape how we view autistic individuals, influencing everything from personal interactions to policymaking. For families navigating the autism spectrum, these myths can distort expectations, fuel stigma, and even hinder access to needed support.

Imagine the impact of hearing a myth and taking it as truth. It can lead to feelings of isolation for autistic individuals, as their reality doesn't match societal expectations. Families might feel pressure to conform to or combat these myths, causing unnecessary stress. The ripple effect of these misunderstandings reaches far, affecting friendships, education, and employment opportunities.

Breaking down these myths isn't just about setting the record straight; it's about tearing down barriers. It's a crucial step towards building a more inclusive society where autistic individuals are recognized for their true selves, not mislabeled by fiction. Through understanding, we pave the way for acceptance, support, and opportunities for autistic individuals to shine on their own terms. Let's dive into some of these common myths and unveil the reality behind them, moving towards a future where autism is understood, not misconstrued.

Myth vs. Reality

Myth 1: Autistic People Don't Feel Emotions Many believe autistic individuals lack the capacity to feel or express emotions. This couldn't be farther from the truth. Autistic people experience the same range of emotions as anyone else; the difference lies in how these emotions are communicated. Some may not express how they feel in ways that are easily recognizable to others, but that doesn't mean the feelings aren't there. Research and personal accounts from autistic individuals highlight that not only do they feel emotions, but they can also be deeply empathetic, often feeling things very intensely.

Myth 2: Autistic Individuals Prefer to Be Alone This myth stems from the observation that some autistic people might seek solitude at times. However, this preference for alone time is not a rejection of social interaction but a way to recharge and process sensory information. The desire for meaningful connections and friendships exists as much in autistic individuals as it does in non-autistic people. The challenge often lies in navigating social cues and finding social settings that are comfortable and accommodating.

Myth 3: Autism is Just a Childhood Disorder Autism is a lifelong condition. The misconception that it only affects children has led to a shortage of support and resources for adults on the spectrum. While some symptoms may change or evolve with age, autistic individuals continue to experience the world differently throughout their lives. It's crucial for support and understanding to extend beyond childhood, offering autistic adults the opportunity to thrive in their personal and professional lives.

Myth 4: Vaccines Cause Autism One of the most damaging myths is the claim that vaccines cause autism. This theory has been thoroughly debunked by numerous studies showing no link between vaccination and the development of autism. The myth originated from a now-discredited study that has caused considerable harm by reducing vaccination rates. Vaccines are an essential part of public health, and there's no evidence to support the claim that they have anything to do with autism.

Myth 5: Autistic People Have the Same Abilities and Challenges Autism is a spectrum, meaning it manifests uniquely in each individual. Grouping all autistic people together overlooks the vast diversity within the autism community. Some may have exceptional abilities in art, mathematics, or memory, while others might face significant challenges in communication or sensory processing. Recognizing the individuality of each autistic person is key to providing the right support and opportunities for growth.

Myth 6: Strict Routines Mean Lack of Flexibility It's commonly thought that autistic individuals adhere to strict routines because they lack flexibility. While routines provide a sense of security and structure, this doesn't mean autistic people are incapable of adapting to change. With the right support and preparation, many can manage changes to their routines. This myth undermines the adaptability and resilience that autistic individuals often show in the face of a world that can be overwhelmingly unpredictable.

By dismantling these myths, we not only foster a deeper understanding of autism but also pave the way for a society that embraces neurodiversity. Each debunked myth brings us closer to recognizing the intrinsic value and potential of every autistic individual, ensuring they are supported, respected, and celebrated for who they are.

Overcoming these myths is crucial for fostering a society that truly understands and accepts autism. Each myth dispelled brings us a step closer to appreciating the rich tapestry of the human experience and recognizing that autistic individuals contribute uniquely and significantly to our world. By challenging misconceptions, we open doors to empathy, support, and opportunities for autistic people, allowing them to live fully and be understood on their own terms.

It's about more than just correcting false beliefs; it's about building a foundation of respect and inclusivity. As we replace myths with reality, we encourage a culture that values diversity, champions individual strengths, and provides the necessary support for autistic individuals to thrive. The journey towards acceptance and understanding begins with us — by acknowledging the truth about autism, we pave the way for a more inclusive and compassionate world.

Understanding Autistic Strengths

In the world of autism, strengths flourish in the most vibrant ways, painting a picture of potential and uniqueness. Too often, conversations about autism focus on the challenges, overlooking the remarkable abilities many autistic individuals possess. Recognizing these strengths is not just about balancing the narrative; it's about seeing the whole person.

Autistic strengths can vary widely, reflecting the diversity of the spectrum itself. From exceptional memory and attention to detail to unique problem-solving abilities and creativity, these strengths offer a glimpse into the extraordinary ways in which autistic minds work. Embracing these abilities provides a foundation for growth, self-esteem, and success. It's about shifting our perspective to appreciate the unique contributions autistic individuals make to our communities and society. By valuing these strengths, we not only support autistic individuals in harnessing their potential but also enrich our collective experience, learning from the diversity of thought and perspective that autism brings.

Understanding and nurturing the strengths of autistic individuals can lead to remarkable outcomes, not just for the individuals themselves but for society. Here, we delve into four specific strengths that are commonly observed among autistic people, along with examples and suggestions for support.

Detail-Oriented Perspectives Many autistic individuals have an incredible ability to notice and recall fine details that others may overlook. This attention to detail can be a significant asset in various fields, including art, science, and technology. For instance, an autistic artist might create exceptionally intricate and realistic drawings, capturing nuances that add depth and life to their work.

Support Suggestions:

- **Encourage hobbies or activities that utilize this strength, such as model building, collecting, or drawing.**

- **Involve them in tasks that require a keen eye for detail, like editing written work or organizing spaces.**

Deep Focus The capacity for deep focus allows many on the spectrum to immerse themselves fully in activities or subjects of interest. This can lead to a high level of expertise and innovation. For example, an autistic individual fascinated by computers might spend hours learning to code, eventually developing a new software application.

Support Suggestions:

- **Provide a quiet, comfortable space where they can concentrate without distractions.**

- **Celebrate their achievements and encourage them to share their interests with others who appreciate their passion.**

Unique Problem-Solving Skills Autistic individuals often approach problems in novel ways, thinking outside the traditional frameworks. This unique perspective can lead to creative solutions that others might not consider. A child on the spectrum might find an unconventional yet effective way to organize a community event, making it more accessible for people with different needs.

Support Suggestions:

- **Involve them in brainstorming sessions for family or community projects.**

- **Offer puzzles, games, and challenges that stimulate their problem-solving skills.**

Intense Passions and Expertise Many autistic people develop deep passions for specific subjects, leading to a profound level of knowledge and expertise. This intense interest can become a foundation for a career or a lifelong hobby that brings joy and satisfaction. For example, an individual with a passion for astronomy might become an advocate for space exploration, sharing their knowledge through writing or public speaking.

Support Suggestions:

- **Provide books, documentaries, and other resources to help them explore their interests further.**

- **Look for clubs, groups, or online communities where they can connect with others who share their passion.**

By recognizing and nurturing these strengths, parents and caregivers can help autistic individuals build confidence and find their place in the world. It's about focusing on what they can do rather than what they can't and providing opportunities for them to shine in their unique way.

Actionable Steps to Nurture and Celebrate Autistic Strengths:

1. **Create a Strengths Journal**: Keep a journal dedicated to noting down your child's strengths and the moments when they shine. Review it regularly with your child, celebrating their abilities and discussing ways these strengths can be applied in daily life and future goals.

2. **Design Strengths-Based Projects**: Tailor activities or projects around your child's specific strengths. For example, if your child has a knack for patterns, consider puzzles or coding games. This not only reinforces their abilities but also boosts their confidence.

3. **Encourage Social Sharing**: Find clubs or groups that align with your child's strengths. Whether it's an art class for creative expression or a science club for analytical thinkers, these environments can be incredibly affirming and supportive.

4. **Advocate for Strengths in Educational Settings**: Work with educators to ensure that your child's learning environment supports and leverages their strengths. This might involve differentiated learning strategies or the inclusion of interests that motivate and engage your child.

5. **Celebrate Small Wins**: Recognize and celebrate achievements that highlight your child's strengths, no matter how small. This could be as simple as completing a challenging puzzle or sharing a creative story. Celebrations can be quiet acknowledgments or shared family moments, reinforcing the value of their unique abilities.

Autism in Boys vs. Girls: Navigating the Differences

Understanding autism's presentation across genders is key to ensuring that all individuals receive the tailored support and intervention they need. Traditionally, autism has been more frequently diagnosed in boys, but this doesn't mean it's less prevalent in girls; rather, it often presents differently, leading to underdiagnosis or misdiagnosis in females. Recognizing these differences is crucial for several reasons. First, it enables parents, educators, and healthcare professionals to identify autism in girls more effectively, ensuring they receive the early support vital for their development.

Second, it highlights the need for gender-specific approaches to intervention that consider the unique challenges and strengths of autistic girls and boys. Lastly, understanding gender differences in autism helps dismantle stereotypes and biases, promoting a more inclusive and supportive environment for everyone on the spectrum. This nuanced approach acknowledges the broad spectrum of autism and the diversity within it, ensuring that every child can thrive.

Exploring the Differences

The journey of understanding autism across genders reveals key distinctions in diagnosis, socialization, and strengths, particularly highlighting the challenge of underdiagnosis in girls. These differences underscore the importance of a nuanced approach to supporting autistic individuals.

Diagnosis: Autism tends to be diagnosed more frequently and earlier in boys, often because they exhibit the classic symptoms recognized by current diagnostic criteria. Girls, however, may display less overt signs of autism or may be more adept at masking their difficulties in social situations. This masking can lead to girls being overlooked or misdiagnosed with conditions such as anxiety or depression, delaying access to autism-specific support.

Socialization: Boys with autism might show more evident social communication challenges, such as difficulty in initiating interactions or a marked disinterest in social engagements. Girls, on the other hand, may mimic social cues and behaviors from peers, a coping strategy that helps them blend in. While this may seem advantageous, it can lead to internal stress and a sense of isolation, as the effort to maintain this facade is taxing and doesn't reflect their genuine social experiences.

Strengths: Autistic boys often excel in areas that involve systemizing or understanding rule-based systems, such as math or computer science. Girls with autism, while also capable in these areas, may show particular strengths in pattern recognition, creativity, and empathy. These skills can manifest in unique artistic talents or a deep understanding of animals and nature, areas where they feel a profound connection.

Underdiagnosis in Girls: The underdiagnosis of autism in girls has significant implications. Without a proper diagnosis, many girls miss out on early interventions that are critical for developing coping strategies and support networks. This oversight can lead to challenges in mental health, self-esteem, and academic achievement. Furthermore, the lack of recognition contributes to a gap in our understanding of autism in girls, perpetuating a cycle of inadequate support and resources.

Addressing these differences requires a shift in how we view and diagnose autism, moving towards a model that recognizes the diverse manifestations of autistic traits across genders. Increasing awareness and understanding among parents, educators, and healthcare professionals is crucial. It ensures that all autistic individuals, regardless of gender, can receive the understanding and support they need to navigate the world on their own terms. This shift not only improves the lives of those on the spectrum but enriches our collective knowledge of the complexity and diversity of the human experience.

Support Strategies

Tailoring support strategies to account for the nuanced differences between genders in autism is essential for providing meaningful and effective assistance. Recognizing and adapting to these variations ensures that each individual receives the personalized care they need to thrive. Here are some strategies that emphasize the importance of an individualized approach:

1. **Gender-Sensitive Diagnostic Tools**: Utilize assessment and diagnostic tools sensitive to gender differences in autism presentation. This includes training professionals to recognize the subtler signs of autism in girls, such as social masking and internalizing behaviors, ensuring earlier and more accurate diagnoses.

2. **Inclusive Social Skills Training**: Develop social skills programs that respect and respond to the different ways boys and girls with autism may experience and navigate social situations. For girls, this might include support for unmasking and expressing their authentic selves in safe environments, while boys might benefit from structured social interactions that build on their interests.

3. **Strength-Based Support**: Identify and nurture the unique strengths of each individual, whether it's a boy's systemizing abilities or a girl's creative and empathetic skills. Encouraging these talents can boost self-esteem and offer pathways to social connection and future career opportunities.

4. **Mental Health Support**: Given the high risk of anxiety and depression, especially among girls who may struggle with social masking, provide targeted mental health support. This should include therapies that address issues related to identity, self-esteem, and coping strategies for managing stress and sensory overload.

5. **Parent and Educator Training**: Educate parents, educators, and caregivers on the diverse presentations of autism across genders. Empower them with the knowledge to recognize and advocate for the needs of autistic children, fostering a supportive and understanding environment at home and in school.

Embracing the unique needs and strengths of all autistic individuals, regardless of gender, enriches our understanding and appreciation of diversity. By recognizing and supporting these differences, we empower every individual on the spectrum to lead a life filled with achievement, fulfillment, and joy. Together, let's celebrate and advocate for the incredible diversity within the autism community.

CHAPTER 3:

THE DIAGNOSIS JOURNEY

When the word "diagnosis" becomes a part of your life, it's natural to feel a mix of emotions. You might be worried, hopeful, or even a bit lost. This chapter is here to walk with you through this new path, holding a lantern to light the way. The goal isn't just to navigate the twists and turns of getting a diagnosis but to understand what it truly means for you and your child. It's about opening doors to support, care, and a community that understands.

Getting a diagnosis for your child can feel like stepping into a new world. This chapter is designed to be your guide, helping you prepare for what's ahead, understand the process, and know what steps to take after you've received the diagnosis. It's not just about labels; it's about understanding your child better and finding the right kind of help and support.

Preparing for the diagnosis is more than just making appointments and ticking boxes. It's about observing your child, understanding the signs, and knowing who to turn to for professional advice. It involves heart work, too — getting ready emotionally for the range of feelings you might experience. This chapter will offer practical advice on how to approach professionals, what signs to look for, and how to ready your heart and mind for the journey.

After the diagnosis, you might wonder, "What now?" We'll explore how to process those initial reactions and what the diagnosis means. It's a chance to see your child's unique strengths and challenges more clearly and to start planning for their future. This part of the chapter will also talk about building your support network — a crucial step in navigating the path ahead.

Lastly, we'll dive into how to navigate healthcare and support systems. This means understanding the therapies and services that can support your child's development, working with schools to ensure they receive the education they deserve, and addressing financial and legal considerations. Here, you'll find clear, actionable advice on accessing services, advocating for your child in educational settings, and managing the practical aspects of care and support.

This chapter aims to be a compassionate guide through the diagnosis process, offering clarity, support, and practical steps. You're not alone on this journey, and with the right knowledge and resources, you can navigate it with confidence and hope.

Preparing for the Diagnosis

Understanding why a diagnosis is vital opens a new chapter in supporting your child's journey. It's about more than a label; it's about understanding your child's unique way of experiencing the world. This knowledge is a key that unlocks a treasure chest of resources and support tailored to their needs.

When your child is diagnosed, you're given a roadmap. This map highlights the specific areas where your child might need extra support and points out their strengths. It helps in tailoring their learning environment, ensuring they have the tools they need to thrive. Services such as speech therapy, occupational therapy, or social skills groups become accessible, each designed to support your child in unique ways.

Moreover, a diagnosis connects you with a community of families navigating similar paths. Within this community, you'll find understanding, support, and shared experiences. This network can be invaluable, providing insights and resources that you might not have found on your own.

Signs and Symptoms to Observe

Recognizing the signs and symptoms of autism early can be a crucial step in getting the support and resources your child needs to flourish. Autism manifests in various ways, and understanding these signs can help you navigate the path toward a diagnosis. Here are key indicators to watch for, categorized into social, communication, and behavioral aspects.

Social Indicators:

- **Limited Eye Contact:** Your child may avoid looking directly at you or others during interactions.

- **Preference for Solitude:** They might prefer playing alone, showing less interest in making friends or interacting with peers.

- **Challenges in Understanding Social Cues:** Difficulty in interpreting body language, facial expressions, or the emotions of others.

Communication Indicators:

- **Delayed Speech Development:** Your child may start talking later than their peers or not use as many words as children of the same age.

- **Echolalia:** Repeating phrases or words heard elsewhere instead of using spontaneous language.

- **Struggles with Conversational Exchange:** They might not respond to their name, have trouble following instructions, or find it hard to express their needs and wants.

Behavioral Indicators:

- **Routine and Structure Dependence:** Your child may become distressed by changes in routine or insist on following specific patterns.

- **Repetitive Behaviors:** Engaging in repetitive movements, such as rocking, spinning, or flapping hands.

- **Intense Focus on Specific Interests:** They might have a deep, intense focus on particular subjects or objects.

These signs are not definitive proof of autism, as each child is unique, and development varies widely. However, if you observe these patterns persistently, it might be beneficial to seek a professional evaluation. This checklist is a starting point meant to guide and support you in understanding your child's needs. Remember, you know your child best, and your observations are valuable in shaping their journey toward growth and development.

Choosing the Right Professionals

Selecting the right professionals for your child's diagnosis journey is like finding guides who can help navigate a forest. You need experts who not only know the terrain well but also understand how to make the journey as comfortable as possible for your child and your family. Developmental pediatricians and child psychologists are two types of professionals who bring their expertise and compassion to the table.

Developmental pediatricians specialize in children's growth and developmental milestones. They have a keen eye for the nuances of development and can provide insights into your child's unique path. Their medical background allows them to consider all aspects of your child's well-being, offering a holistic approach to diagnosis and support.

Child psychologists, on the other hand, delve into the social and emotional aspects of your child's development. They are adept at understanding how children communicate and interact with the world around them. Through observation and interaction, they can uncover the layers of your child's experiences, providing clarity on their needs and strengths.

When choosing the right professional, look for someone who not only has the credentials but also demonstrates a deep understanding of and respect for autism's spectrum. Their approach should resonate with your family's values and your child's comfort. Trust your instincts; the right professional should make you feel heard, supported, and hopeful.

Emotional Preparation

Preparing yourself emotionally for your child's diagnosis process is as important as gathering all the necessary information. This emotional journey might take you through a spectrum of feelings, from hope to anxiety and everything in between. Recognizing and accepting these emotions as part of the process is the first step toward preparing yourself.

Begin by acknowledging that it's okay to have a mix of feelings. There's no right or wrong way to feel. You might find yourself swinging between optimism about finally understanding your child's unique needs and worries about the challenges ahead. Allow yourself this space to feel without judgment.

Managing expectations is crucial. While it's natural to hope for clear answers and a straightforward path, the reality can be more complex. Understanding that the diagnosis is just the beginning of a longer journey can help temper expectations. It's about equipping yourself with knowledge and support, not about finding a quick fix.

Seeking support from loved ones or connecting with other parents who have gone through similar experiences can be incredibly grounding. Sharing your thoughts and emotions with someone who understands can provide comfort and reassurance.

Remember, preparing emotionally is not about bracing for the worst but about steadying yourself for the insights and understanding that the diagnosis process can bring. This preparation is an act of love and strength, setting a foundation of resilience and hope for your family's journey ahead.

Beyond the Label: What Comes Next?

Receiving an autism diagnosis for your child can evoke a complex blend of emotions. It's common to feel a rush of relief at having an explanation for your child's unique behaviors and challenges. This relief, however, might quickly mingle with worry, sadness, or even a sense of loss. Such feelings are natural and valid, reflecting the deep love and concern you have for your child's well-being and future.

As you navigate these initial reactions, it's important to give yourself permission to feel everything without rushing to judgment or immediate action. Emotions can be like waves, ebbing and flowing with intensity over time. Acknowledge each feeling as it comes, knowing that this emotional landscape is part of many parents' experiences when they receive significant news about their child.

Seeking support during this time can be invaluable. Connecting with other parents who have walked this path can offer perspective and understanding. Professional guidance, whether from a therapist, a counselor, or a support group, can provide strategies for coping with and processing these emotions.

Remember, an autism diagnosis is a starting point, not an endpoint. It opens up avenues for support, understanding, and growth. As you move beyond the initial emotions, you'll find pathways to celebrate your child's uniqueness and strengths, crafting a journey that's rich, fulfilling, and full of potential.

Understanding the diagnosis of autism is like receiving a key to a previously locked door. It reveals a room filled with insights into your child's unique way of experiencing the world. This understanding is crucial, not just for navigating the challenges but also for appreciating the strengths that come with being on the autism spectrum.

Autism is often described as a spectrum because it encompasses a wide range of abilities and challenges. No two children on the spectrum are the same; each has their own distinctive set of skills, interests, and areas where they may need support. Some children might have remarkable abilities in music, art, mathematics, or memory. Others may excel in pattern recognition, have a rich vocabulary, or show an incredible understanding of particular subjects.

However, challenges exist alongside these strengths. Your child may find social interactions puzzling, experience sensory sensitivities, or face difficulties with traditional communication methods. It's important to remember that these challenges do not define your child but are simply aspects of their journey that require understanding and support.

A diagnosis helps tailor this support, guiding you toward strategies, therapies, and environments that enhance your child's development. It also helps in advocating for your child in educational settings, ensuring they receive the accommodations necessary to thrive.

Understanding your child's diagnosis is an ongoing process. As they grow and change, you'll discover more about their needs, abilities, and how they see the world. Embracing the spectrum nature of autism means celebrating your child's unique perspective, fostering their strengths, and supporting them through their challenges. This balanced view can transform the diagnosis from a label into a powerful tool for empowerment and growth.

Planning for the Future

With a diagnosis in hand, planning for your child's future becomes a journey of hope and action. Understanding your child's unique strengths and challenges is the compass that guides this journey. It's crucial to set realistic goals and expectations, ones that honor their individuality and potential. These goals might range from developing communication skills to nurturing social connections or fostering independence according to their abilities and interests.

Early intervention is key. It's like planting a seed and nurturing it with the right conditions to grow; the earlier you start, the stronger the foundation you lay for your child's development. These interventions, tailored to meet your child's specific needs, can significantly impact their ability to interact with the world around them. They are not about changing who your child is but about giving them the tools to navigate their environment confidently.

As you plan, remember to celebrate the small victories along the way. Each milestone, no matter how small it may seem, is a testament to your child's growth and your support. Setting realistic goals doesn't mean limiting your child's potential; it means moving forward with a clear, hopeful perspective, ready to embrace every success and tackle every challenge with love and determination.

Building a Support Network

Creating a robust support network is like weaving a safety net that catches you and your family during challenging times and lifts you during moments of triumph. This network is not just about finding the right professionals to support your child's development but also about connecting with people who understand your journey on a personal level.

Reaching out to other parents and caregivers who are on a similar path can be incredibly grounding. These connections often turn into lifelong friendships, offering mutual understanding, advice, and a listening ear when needed. Autism support groups, both in person and online, serve as vital platforms for sharing experiences, resources, and strategies that have worked for others facing similar challenges.

In today's digital age, online resources are invaluable. The internet is a treasure trove of information and support, from forums and social media groups to educational websites and webinars. These resources can help you stay informed about the latest research, therapies, and advocacy efforts. They also offer flexibility, allowing you to connect with others and access support from the comfort of your home, on your schedule.

Building this network takes time, but the effort is worth it. Each connection adds another strand to your safety net, ensuring that when you need support, advice, or simply someone to talk to, you're not alone. This network becomes a community, one that understands, supports, and journeys with you every step of the way.

Navigating Healthcare and Support Systems

Embarking on the journey to access services and therapies for your child can be transformative. Here's a guide to understanding and obtaining the support your child needs:

- **Speech Therapy:** This therapy enhances communication skills, which is crucial for expressing needs and emotions. Whether your child is non-verbal or struggles with effective communication, speech therapists tailor strategies to improve their ability to interact with others.

- **Occupational Therapy (OT):** OT focuses on developing essential life skills, from fine motor skills for writing to daily tasks like dressing. Occupational therapists work on sensory integration, coordination, and self-care skills, fostering independence in children.

- **Applied Behavior Analysis (ABA) Therapy:** ABA therapy targets social, communication, and learning skills through positive reinforcement. It's adaptable to each child's needs, making learning more effective and enjoyable.

Accessing These Services:

1. **Consult Your Pediatrician:** Begin with your child's doctor, who can provide referrals to specialists in speech, occupational, and ABA therapies.

2. **Insurance and Funding:** Check with your insurance provider for coverage details. Explore public assistance programs for additional support.

   Note: In the UK, the National Health Service (NHS) provides coverage for many therapies and services, reducing reliance on private insurance. However, additional funding sources and grants may still be available to supplement NHS support.

3. **Local and Online Support Groups:** Engage with communities for personal recommendations and experiences with different therapies.

4. **School Resources:** Schools often have connections with local therapists and may offer services directly.

Case Study for Success: Emma's parents noticed her difficulty with communication at age three. After consulting their pediatrician, they were referred to a speech therapist covered by their insurance. Through bi-weekly sessions and home exercises, Emma made significant progress in expressing her needs and engaging with her family.

This structured approach to accessing services ensures that you can find the right support for your child, helping them thrive in communication, daily activities, and social interactions.

Working with Schools and Educational Systems

Partnering with your child's school is a key step in ensuring they receive the education and support suited to their unique needs. Individualized Education Programs (IEPs) and 504 plans are two pivotal tools in this partnership, designed to provide tailored educational strategies and accommodations. Here's how to navigate these important processes:

- **Understand Your Rights:** Familiarize yourself with your child's rights under the Individuals with Disabilities Education Act (IDEA) for IEPs and Section 504 of the Rehabilitation Act for 504 plans. Knowing these can empower you to advocate effectively.

- **Open Communication:** Establish a proactive and collaborative relationship with teachers, school psychologists, and administrators. Regular communication is essential for sharing insights about your child's needs and progress.

- **Gather Documentation:** Compile a comprehensive file of evaluations, reports, and doctor's notes that detail your child's diagnosis and needs. This documentation will support your case for specific accommodations or services.

- **Be Specific:** Clearly articulate the accommodations or interventions your child needs to succeed. Whether it's extra time on tests, a quiet space for exams, or therapy services, specificity helps the school understand and meet your child's needs.

- **Seek Support:** Don't hesitate to seek advice from other parents, support groups, or educational advocates who have experience with IEPs and 504 plans. They can offer valuable guidance and support throughout the process.

- **Follow Up:** After the IEP or 504 plan is in place, regularly monitor your child's progress and the implementation of accommodations. Open lines of communication with educators allow for adjustments as your child's needs evolve.

Working collaboratively with educational systems ensures your child receives the support they deserve, paving the way for a successful and inclusive educational experience.

Navigating the financial and legal landscape of autism support requires a blend of planning, understanding, and advocacy. Here's how to approach these crucial areas:

Financial Planning: Early and thoughtful financial planning can provide a stable foundation for your child's needs. Consider setting up a special needs trust or savings account specifically designed for individuals with disabilities, such as an ABLE account. These financial tools can help manage the costs associated with therapies, educational supports, and future living expenses without jeopardizing eligibility for government benefits.

Insurance Matters: Understanding your insurance coverage is key. Many insurance plans are required to cover essential services for autism, including therapies like ABA, occupational, and speech therapy. Review your policy details, and don't hesitate to challenge denials or discrepancies. State laws vary, so familiarize yourself with your state's mandates on autism coverage.

Note: *In the UK, the NHS provides coverage for many therapies and services, significantly reducing the reliance on private insurance. However, supplementary private insurance may still offer benefits not covered by the NHS.*

Legal Rights: Familiarize yourself with the legal protections and rights afforded to your child. The Individuals with Disabilities Education Act (IDEA) ensures the right to a free and appropriate public education in the least restrictive environment. This may include access to an Individualized Education Program (IEP) or a 504 Plan, which provides tailored educational support and accommodations. Understanding these rights is essential for advocating effectively for your child.

In each of these areas, seeking advice from professionals, such as financial advisors familiar with special needs planning, insurance experts, or special education attorneys, can be incredibly beneficial. Additionally, many non-profit organizations offer resources and guidance to help families navigate these complex systems. Remember, proactive planning and informed advocacy are your tools in ensuring your child has access to the services and support they need to thrive.

SECTION 2:

SOCIAL
COMMUNICATION
& INTERACTION

CHAPTER 4:

BUILDING BRIDGES OF COMMUNICATION

Words are not the only way we talk to each other. For many autistic children, non-verbal cues — like gestures, facial expressions, and the way they move — are their main way of sharing how they feel and what they need. This silent form of chatting can say a lot. Think of it as a secret code, unique to every child, waiting to be understood.

For kids who find words tricky, these signals can help them tell their story. It's like when you can tell a friend is upset just by the way they slump into a chair. With autistic children, noticing and understanding these silent messages is even more crucial. It opens up a window into their world, showing us not just their needs and feelings but also their likes, dislikes, and how they relate to the world around them.

By tuning into this silent language, we start to build a bridge of understanding and connection. It's not always easy, and it can take some time to learn this special code. But the effort is worth it. It brings us closer, breaking down walls and letting us see the world through their eyes. This chapter will guide you through this world of unspoken words, offering tools to decode, respond to, and support your child's non-verbal communication. Through learning and practice, you'll find new ways to connect, support, and celebrate your child's unique way of expressing themselves.

Understanding Non-Verbal Signals

Non-verbal communication holds a special place in the hearts and lives of autistic children. Many of these remarkable young individuals communicate their thoughts, feelings, and needs without saying a word. Instead, they use a rich tapestry of gestures, facial expressions, and movements. These are their words, their letters, and their sentences, painting a vivid picture of their inner world for those who know how to read them.

For a child who finds the bustling world of spoken language challenging, these non-verbal cues become their voice. This silent language can convey a wealth of information — from joy and frustration to the need for solitude or connection. Recognizing and understanding this form of communication is not just beneficial; it's essential. It's a bridge to understanding the unique perspectives and needs of autistic children, providing a foundation for deeper connection and mutual understanding.

In the following sections, we will explore the landscape of non-verbal communication among autistic children. We'll learn to recognize and interpret these silent signals and discover ways to support and respond to them. Through real-life examples, we'll see how this understanding transforms relationships, fostering a nurturing environment where every child can thrive.

Recognizing and Interpreting Signals

Supporting your child's non-verbal communication is a journey of learning and adaptation, a way of tuning into a frequency that's often overlooked but immensely powerful. The key lies in creating a space where your child feels understood and respected, using tools and strategies that align with their unique way of expressing themselves.

Visual aids can be a game-changer in this process. Picture cards, for example, allow children to express their needs, feelings, or choices without the pressure of finding the right words. They can point to a picture of a glass of water or a favorite toy, bridging the gap between their inner world and the world around them. Similarly, schedules with symbols or images can help them understand the day's routine, reducing anxiety and building confidence.

Gesture-based communication is another invaluable tool. Simple signs or gestures for "more," "stop," or "I love you" can be easily learned and used by both you and your child, creating a private language that's both empowering and inclusive. This doesn't replace speech but enriches the ways in which you connect and understand each other.

Patience and observation are perhaps the most crucial elements. Learning to read your child's non-verbal cues takes time and attention. It's about noticing the small changes in posture, the flickers of emotion across their face, or the patterns in their stimming behaviors. Each of these is a piece of the puzzle, offering insights into their feelings and needs.

In one family, the breakthrough came when a mother noticed her son's fascination with spinning objects. She introduced a spinner as a way for him to indicate wanting to play. Soon, he would bring the spinner to her whenever he felt playful, a simple act that became their first step towards deeper communication.

Another example is a father who realized his daughter squeezed her hands tightly when feeling overwhelmed. Recognizing this cue, he introduced a soft stress ball for her to squeeze instead. This not only helped her manage her feelings but also became a signal for him to provide comfort and a quiet space, strengthening their bond without a word being spoken.

These stories highlight the profound impact of tuning into and supporting non-verbal communication, showcasing the transformative power of understanding and responding to the unspoken.

Techniques to Enhance Verbal Communication

Opening the doors to verbal communication for autistic children can be like finding the key to a hidden garden. It's a place where thoughts, needs, and emotions can blossom into words, offering a new way to connect with the world.

However, for many autistic children, these doors don't open easily. Words can get tangled, the flow of conversation can be puzzling, and the nuances of language can seem out of reach. This isn't about a lack of desire to communicate but rather the challenges in navigating the complexities of verbal expression.

The beauty of speech lies not just in the ability to convey basic needs but in sharing one's thoughts, feelings, and personality. For children on the autism spectrum, the journey to verbal communication can be varied and full of twists. Some may find their voice early on, while others may take more time to express themselves through words.

The challenges are real, but so are the possibilities. With patience, understanding, and the right strategies, we can support these children in unlocking their verbal potential, enriching their interactions, and helping them share their unique perspectives with the world. In the following sections, we'll explore practical techniques to nurture and enhance verbal communication, opening up new avenues for expression and connection.

Fostering verbal communication begins with the foundation: simplicity, clarity, and the art of listening. These fundamental strategies create a supportive environment that encourages autistic children to express themselves verbally, making the process less daunting and more engaging.

Simplify Language: The world is a bustling marketplace of words and sounds, where simplicity can be the guiding light. For autistic children, breaking down language into its simplest form can help demystify the complex world of verbal communication.

Use words that are direct and easy to understand. This doesn't mean talking down to them; it means talking with them in a way that they can grasp and respond to, creating a bridge between their thoughts and the words they wish to express.

Clear and Concise Sentences: Like carefully laid stones in a garden path, clear and concise sentences can guide a child through the landscape of language. Long, winding sentences can be confusing, making it harder for children to follow along or respond. Instead, short sentences provide clear directions and make it easier for children to process information and formulate their own responses. This clarity not only aids in understanding but also in building the child's confidence in their ability to communicate.

Active Listening: Listening is the soil from which understanding grows. Active listening involves giving full attention, showing that you value what the child says, and responding in a way that affirms their efforts. This means being patient, waiting for them to finish their thoughts, and resisting the urge to correct every mispronunciation or grammatical error. It's about acknowledging their attempts, encouraging their progress, and letting them know that their voice is heard and valued.

By embedding these basic communication strategies into daily interactions, parents and caregivers can create a nurturing environment that supports the growth of verbal communication skills, paving the way for richer, more meaningful conversations.

Advanced Techniques for Enhancing Verbal Interaction

As we dive deeper into the world of verbal communication, exploring advanced strategies can open new doors for our children to express themselves. These approaches build on the foundational techniques, introducing innovative ways to enrich interactions and strengthen the bridge between thoughts and spoken words.

Technology aids have become invaluable in this journey. Speech-generating devices and apps can give a voice to those who find verbal communication challenging. These tools are not just about providing words but about offering choices, enabling children to construct sentences, share their ideas, and participate in conversations. They serve as stepping stones, building confidence and skills that can transition into more spontaneous verbal communication.

Speech therapy exercises tailored to the individual needs of autistic children can also play a critical role. Through fun and engaging activities, children can work on articulation, turn-taking, and understanding the flow of conversation. These exercises are not one-size-fits-all; they're carefully crafted to resonate with each child's unique interests and strengths. For example, incorporating a child's love for animals into therapy can transform a session into an exciting adventure, where every new word is a discovery.

Incorporating interests into conversations is another powerful technique. When we talk about what excites our children, their motivation to engage verbally can skyrocket. This approach not only makes communication more enjoyable but also more meaningful. It turns abstract concepts into tangible topics, weaving the child's passions into the fabric of the conversation.

These advanced techniques, when applied with patience and creativity, can significantly enhance verbal interaction. They offer pathways for our children to share their thoughts and feelings, bringing us closer to understanding their world and enriching our collective experience.

Encouraging Progress

In the journey of enhancing verbal communication, embracing patience and celebrating every small victory play pivotal roles. These moments, as minor as they might seem, are monumental steps forward for a child with autism. Recognizing and cheering each word, attempt at speech, or non-verbal communication effort reinforces their confidence and motivates further progress. It's a process that flourishes in an environment of support and understanding, where attempts at communication are met with encouragement rather than correction.

Creating such a nurturing environment means acknowledging the immense courage it takes for these children to try verbal expression. Every attempt, whether successful or not, is a triumph. It's about more than just the words; it's about the effort, the intention, and the bravery to reach out and connect. This approach fosters a safe space where children feel valued and understood, encouraging them to continue exploring and expanding their verbal abilities without the fear of judgment.

Patience is the cornerstone of this process. It reminds us that progress is not measured by the speed but by the growth and resilience demonstrated along the way. In this light, every word uttered and every attempt to communicate becomes a cause for celebration, a milestone in their developmental journey. By focusing on these achievements, we not only bolster their confidence but also cement the foundation for continued growth in verbal communication.

Encouraging Social Interaction: Tips and Tricks

Social interaction is a vital part of human connection, offering a mirror through which we see ourselves reflected in the world around us. For autistic children, however, navigating social landscapes presents unique challenges. These young explorers may find social cues perplexing, group dynamics overwhelming, and the ebb and flow of conversation hard to follow. Yet, the value of forging connections with others cannot be overstated — it's through these interactions that children learn, grow, and discover their place in the world.

Emphasizing the importance of social interaction doesn't mean forcing conformity to typical social norms but rather fostering environments where autistic children can engage in meaningful ways. It's about understanding and appreciating the diversity of communication and interaction styles. By recognizing these challenges, we can tailor our approach, ensuring that each child has the opportunity to develop social skills at their own pace in ways that resonate with them. This section will share practical tips and strategies to support autistic children in embracing social interaction, enriching their experience and understanding of the intricate dance of human connection.

Creating Safe Social Opportunities

Navigating social waters can be daunting for autistic children, who may feel overwhelmed by the unspoken rules and sensory demands of typical social settings. The key to encouraging meaningful social interaction lies in creating and finding safe, supportive environments where these children can feel at ease while engaging with peers. Such spaces allow them to practice social skills without the fear of judgment, fostering a sense of belonging and acceptance.

One effective strategy is seeking out or establishing playgroups focused on shared interests or activities. Whether it's a love for drawing, building with blocks, or exploring nature, these interest-based groups provide a common ground for interaction. In these settings, conversations and collaborations can naturally evolve around a shared focal point, making social exchanges more manageable and meaningful.

Special interest clubs, whether in schools or the community, serve a similar purpose. They offer structured environments where autistic children can explore their passions alongside peers, promoting social connections through mutual enthusiasm. For instance, a robotics club or a gardening group can become a thriving social network for a child who might otherwise feel isolated.

Inclusive sports teams present another valuable opportunity. Sports such as swimming, martial arts, or even team games adapted for inclusivity can promote teamwork, communication, and a sense of achievement. The key is to choose activities that match the child's interests and sensory preferences, ensuring a positive and rewarding experience.

By prioritizing safe, understanding, and interest-driven environments, we create opportunities for autistic children to navigate social interactions on their terms. This approach not only supports their social development but also boosts their confidence, laying the groundwork for a more socially connected life.

Practical Tips for Parents and Caregivers

Facilitating social interactions for autistic children requires creativity, patience, and a bit of strategy. Here are some practical tips to help parents and caregivers create opportunities for meaningful social engagement:

- **Role-Playing**: Use role-playing games to practice social scenarios in a controlled, comfortable setting. This can include greeting someone, taking turns in conversation, or asking for help. It's a fun way to learn and understand social norms and expectations.

- **Social Stories**: Create social stories that depict various social situations and the appropriate responses or behaviors in those scenarios. These stories can help children understand complex social cues and how to navigate them effectively.

- **Visual Supports**: Prepare for social interactions using visual supports like cue cards or visual schedules. These can outline the steps involved in a social activity or provide reminders about social rules.

- **Interest-Based Activities**: Encourage participation in group activities or clubs that align with your child's interests. Shared interests can be a natural icebreaker, making social interactions more engaging and less daunting.

- **Positive Reinforcement**: Offer praise and rewards for attempts at social interaction, no matter how small. This can boost confidence and motivate further attempts at social engagement.

- **Teach Empathy**: Use stories, videos, and real-life examples to teach empathy and the importance of understanding others' feelings and perspectives.

- **Small Group Settings**: Start with small groups or one-on-one playdates to gradually build social comfort and skills. Large groups can be overwhelming and may hinder rather than help social growth.

Implementing these tips can help autistic children gradually build the skills and confidence needed for successful social interactions, fostering a sense of belonging and connection.

Supporting Peer Interactions

Building peer relationships is crucial for the social development of autistic children, yet it often requires thoughtful support and collaboration. Here's how to foster these important connections:

- **Collaborate with Educators**: Work closely with your child's teachers and school staff to identify potential peer buddies who show empathy and an interest in forming friendships. Schools can facilitate interactions through structured activities or buddy systems.

- **Organize Inclusive Activities**: Plan playdates or activities that cater to shared interests between your child and potential friends. Activities that minimize pressure and focus on enjoyment encourage natural interaction and bonding.

- **Educate Peers and Parents**: Educate peers and their parents about autism, emphasizing the strengths and challenges. Understanding and acceptance from both children and adults pave the way for genuine friendships.

- **Foster a Supportive Environment**: Encourage environments where all children are valued and differences are celebrated. Supportive and inclusive settings not only benefit autistic children but enrich the lives of all participants, fostering a community of understanding and empathy.

- **Encourage Communication**: Teach and encourage ways for your child to communicate their needs and interests to peers, whether verbally or through alternative communication methods. This empowers them to take an active role in their social interactions.

By taking these steps, you can help your child navigate the complexities of peer relationships and lay the foundation for meaningful and lasting friendships.

CHAPTER 5

IN THEIR OWN WORLD

⦿⟨⦿⟩⦿

Welcome to a chapter that opens doors to seeing the world through the eyes of autistic children. These amazing young individuals experience life in vibrant, unique ways, especially when it comes to their personal space, the joy of play, and the art of making friends. Each child is a world unto themselves, with distinct preferences, needs, and ways of learning. Our aim here is not just to understand these differences but to celebrate and support them.

For autistic children, personal space is more than a comfort — it's a necessity. Imagine a bubble that surrounds them, a safe haven where they can be themselves, free from overwhelming sensations or unexpected intrusions. Recognizing when and why a child cherishes this personal bubble is the first step toward nurturing their well-being.

Then, there's play — a universal language of learning and expression. For autistic children, play isn't just fun; it's a critical tool for exploring social cues, solving puzzles of interaction, and stretching their creative muscles. But not all play is the same. Each type, from solitary adventures to cooperative missions, serves a unique role in a child's social and emotional development.

And what about making friends? Friendships for autistic children might look different, but the connections are just as deep and meaningful. Here, we'll uncover how these friendships blossom and how parents can cultivate environments where these special bonds can thrive.

Through understanding and supporting these aspects of their world, we empower autistic children to navigate their surroundings with confidence, building a foundation for lifelong learning, meaningful relationships, and heartfelt connections. Let's dive in and explore how we can make their world — a world where every child feels understood, valued, and connected — a better place for them.

Respecting Personal Space and Boundaries

Many autistic children hold their personal space dear, treating it as a sanctuary that shields them from the bustling, often overwhelming world outside. This cherished space is not about isolation; it's about creating a comfort zone where sensations, emotions, and interactions can be processed at their own pace. Intruding into this personal haven can be startling and distressing, leading to anxiety or discomfort.

Why is personal space so important to these children? Imagine navigating a world where sounds, lights, and touches are amplified tenfold. For autistic children, this heightened sensitivity turns their personal space into a crucial buffer — a way to manage the sensory inputs that bombard them daily. Recognizing and respecting this need is paramount.

How can you tell when a child is seeking the refuge of their personal space? Watch for cues: turning away, retreating to a corner, or immersing themselves in a solitary activity. These signals are not acts of rejection but a communication of their current capacity to engage. They're saying, "I need a moment to myself."

Acknowledging these signs by allowing them the space they seek is an essential step in understanding and supporting their unique ways of experiencing the world. By doing so, we foster a sense of security and respect that is foundational for their growth and happiness.

Teaching and Respecting Boundaries

Creating a world where autistic children feel understood begins with teaching them how to express their need for personal space and ensuring others honor these boundaries. Communication is key, but it doesn't always have to be verbal. Simple signals, gestures, or even visual cues can serve as powerful tools for children to convey their need for space.

Start by introducing the concept of personal space with clear, visual examples. Use a favorite toy or a drawing to explain the idea of a "bubble" around each person that needs respect. Encourage your child to show you when they need their bubble to be bigger, perhaps with a hand signal or a special card they can hold up. This empowers them to communicate their needs in a way that feels natural and comfortable to them.

Equally important is teaching siblings, family members, and friends about these boundaries. Gentle reminders and role-playing games can be effective ways to demonstrate how to recognize and respect someone's personal space. This not only supports the autistic child but also fosters a nurturing environment that values and respects individual needs.

Creating a safe space at home where your child can retreat is also crucial. This could be a quiet corner of a room, a cozy nook filled with their favorite books, or a small tent where they can hide away. This designated space serves as a sanctuary where they can unwind, recharge, and process their day. By honoring their need for solitude, you reinforce the message that their feelings and needs are important, validating their right to personal space and autonomy.

Encouraging Independence within Safe Limits

Fostering independence in autistic children is a delicate balance between respecting their personal space and encouraging them to explore their autonomy. The goal is to create an environment that says, "Your space is yours to control, but the world outside it is yours to discover." Offering structured choices is a wonderful way to achieve this balance. This approach allows children to safely express their preferences, whether it's choosing between two activities, what to wear, or which snack they'd like. These decisions empower them, providing a sense of control over their environment and their interactions with it.

Structured choices also teach decision-making and problem-solving skills within the comfort and safety of their personal boundaries. By framing options within clear, manageable limits, you help reduce the anxiety that comes with too many open-ended choices. This method respects their need for predictability and routine while gently nudging them toward independence.

Moreover, structured choices can be a leap to more significant decisions and independence. Start with small choices and gradually increase the complexity as your child becomes more comfortable and confident. Celebrate their choices, reinforcing the notion that their preferences matter and that they have the power to shape their own experiences.

In doing so, we not only respect their personal space but also encourage a journey toward autonomy, crafting a path that lets them navigate the world at their own pace, with confidence and a sense of security.

The Role of Play in Social Learning

Play isn't just a way to pass time; it's a crucial part of growing up. For autistic children, it becomes even more significant. Through play, they learn about the world around them, understand social cues, solve problems, and let their creativity soar. Play is a safe and natural way for them to explore their environment, interact with others, and express themselves. It's through this joyful exploration that they pick up essential life skills, from cooperating with others to understanding emotions and developing empathy.

Engaging in play allows autistic children to learn in a stress-free environment. It's during these moments of fun that they can experiment with social interactions at their own pace. Whether it's taking turns, sharing toys, or navigating the complexities of friendship, play offers a gentle introduction to these concepts. It also provides endless opportunities for problem-solving, whether figuring out how to build a tower from blocks or deciding how to share space and resources in a group game.

Moreover, play is a powerful outlet for creativity. Autistic children often have unique perspectives on the world, and play gives them the space to express these views. Through imaginative play, they can explore different scenarios, roles, and ideas, all of which contribute to their cognitive and emotional development.

Incorporating a variety of play activities is key to supporting an autistic child's social learning. From solitary play that fosters independence and problem-solving to cooperative games that build social skills and teamwork, each type of play contributes to a child's overall development. Activities like puzzles, building blocks, and art projects can stimulate an autistic child's problem-solving skills and creativity, while structured games and social stories can help them understand and practice social cues and interactions.

By embracing the natural learning opportunities that play offers, we can support autistic children in developing the skills they need to navigate social situations, express their creativity, and solve problems. Play isn't just fun; it's foundational to learning and growth.

Types of Play for Different Stages

Play evolves as children grow, each stage building on the last, shaping their understanding of the world and how they interact with it. For autistic children, recognizing and supporting these stages with appropriate activities can significantly enhance their social learning and development.

Solitary Play: Often the starting point, solitary play allows children to explore and interact with their environment on their own terms. It's crucial for developing independence, imagination, and self-soothing techniques. Activities like puzzles, drawing, and playing with sensory toys not only entertain but also stimulate cognitive growth and fine motor skills. For autistic children, solitary play can be a peaceful time to engage deeply with interests and practice self-regulation.

Parallel Play: This stage sees children playing alongside others without direct interaction. It's an essential step towards social play, helping children get used to the presence of peers and observe social norms in a low-pressure environment. Setting up parallel play stations with similar toys in a shared space can encourage this type of play. It's an opportunity for autistic children to become comfortable with others nearby, laying the groundwork for more interactive play later on.

Associative Play: As children begin to interact more during play, they engage in associative play. They may share toys or discuss their activities without organizing their play around a common goal. For autistic children, this stage helps in practicing communication and sharing skills. Simple group activities like a shared art project or playing in a sandbox where they can interact casually over shared materials support this development stage.

Cooperative Play: This advanced stage involves children playing together towards a common goal, requiring negotiation, role assignment, and teamwork. Cooperative play teaches problem-solving, empathy, and social cues. Games with clear rules, team sports, or collaborative storytelling games can encourage this type of interaction. For autistic children, structured activities with clear roles and expectations can make cooperative play more accessible, teaching them valuable lessons in teamwork and social interaction.

By understanding and supporting these stages of play, parents and caregivers can offer activities that not only match their children's developmental needs but also challenge them to grow. Each stage offers unique opportunities for learning and development, making play a powerful tool in the social education of autistic children.

Facilitating Engaging Play Experiences

Creating an environment that nurtures engaging play experiences is essential for the development of autistic children. Such environments not only encourage interaction and learning but also respect the child's individual pace and interests. Here's how you can set up a play space that promotes social skills and meaningful engagement:

1. **Choose the Right Toys and Games:** Select toys that naturally encourage interaction and teamwork. Games that

require taking turns, such as board games or card games, can teach patience and understanding. Toys that can be used in multiple ways, like blocks or art supplies, inspire creativity and offer opportunities for cooperative play.

2. **Create a Safe and Comfortable Space:** Ensure the play area is safe and inviting, with ample room for movement and exploration. Soft lighting, minimal noise, and comfortable seating can make the space more appealing to autistic children, who may be sensitive to sensory inputs.

3. **Incorporate Interests and Strengths:** Tailor the play environment to include elements that match the child's interests and strengths. This personal touch can significantly increase their engagement and enjoyment, making learning through play an enjoyable experience.

4. **Encourage Small Group Interactions:** Organize playdates or small group activities with peers who have similar interests. This setting can foster friendships and social skills in a controlled, manageable environment.

5. **Model Playful Interactions:** Demonstrate how to play and interact with others. Autistic children often learn best through observation. Showing them how to use toys, share with others, and participate in games can provide them with a clear example to follow.

By carefully setting up play environments that cater to the needs and preferences of autistic children, you can create a foundation for rich, engaging play experiences. These settings not only support the development of social skills but also offer children the joy of playing on their terms, fostering a sense of independence and confidence.

Role of Parents and Caregivers in Play

Parents and caregivers play a pivotal role in enriching play experiences for autistic children. By actively participating in play, they not only offer guidance and support but also model social interactions and behaviors. To be effective play partners, it's important to follow the child's lead, showing interest in their activities and adding variations to stimulate creativity and learning.

Simultaneously, encouraging independent play is crucial for developing autonomy. Introduce new toys or games gradually, allowing the child to explore on their own while being available to join in or help as needed. This balance nurtures both social skills and self-reliance, making play a valuable tool for growth.

Making Friends: Strategies for Parents and Children

Understanding Friendship for Autistic Children

Navigating the realm of friendships presents unique challenges for autistic children. Their experiences with forming connections often differ significantly from their peers, not due to a lack of desire for friendship but because of the distinct way they perceive and interact with the world. Autistic children might find the unspoken rules of social interactions puzzling, which can make the process of making friends seem daunting.

However, the value of friendship, even just one close friend, cannot be overstated. Friends provide companionship, understanding, and an opportunity to share interests and experiences. For autistic children, a single friendship can be a profound source of joy and learning, offering a safe space to practice social skills and forge a deep connection based on acceptance and mutual respect.

It's essential to recognize the diversity in social preferences among autistic children. While some may seek numerous friendships, others may feel content with a few or even one meaningful relationship. The key is to honor these individual needs and preferences, supporting autistic children in their journey toward friendship in a way that feels comfortable and rewarding for them.

Empowering autistic children and their families with strategies to navigate these challenges is crucial. By providing tools and understanding, we can help them build fulfilling friendships that enrich their lives and foster a sense of belonging. This journey toward friendship, though it may take various forms, is a testament to the resilience, uniqueness, and depth of autistic individuals.

Strategies for Parents

Fostering friendships for autistic children involves thoughtful consideration and support from parents. The goal is to create opportunities for meaningful connections while respecting the child's comfort and pace. Here's how parents can actively support their children in making and maintaining friendships:

1. **Choose the Right Settings:** Look for social environments that match your child's interests and sensory preferences. Small, structured activities or groups centered around a particular

hobby or interest can be less overwhelming and more engaging for autistic children. Libraries, community centers, and special interest clubs often offer such opportunities.

2. **Facilitate Introductions:** Helping your child navigate the initial stages of friendship can make a significant difference. Introduce them to potential friends with similar interests and ages. Preparing them in advance with information about the other child and suggesting common topics to talk about can ease anxiety and foster a smoother interaction.

3. **Teach Social Norms and Cues:** Use stories, role-playing, or visual aids to teach your child about social cues and norms. Discuss scenarios they might encounter and practice responses or actions they can take. Highlighting the importance of listening, sharing, and taking turns can also prepare them for positive social interactions.

4. **Encourage Empathy and Perspective-Taking:** Teaching your child to consider others' feelings and viewpoints is crucial for building strong friendships. Use real-life situations or stories to discuss different perspectives and emotions, helping your child to develop empathy and understanding.

5. **Provide Ongoing Support:** Be there to listen, offer advice, and celebrate successes. Encourage your child to talk about their social experiences, offering gentle guidance when needed. Recognize and praise their efforts to engage with others, reinforcing the value of persistence and positive social interactions.

By adopting these strategies, parents can create a supportive framework that encourages autistic children to explore friendships, learn social skills, and enjoy the enriching experiences that come with making friends.

Strategies for Children

Making friends can seem like a big task, but with some simple strategies, it becomes much easier. For children, especially those on the autism spectrum, knowing how to start interactions, join in play, and keep friends is invaluable. Here are a few strategies to help:

1. **Start with a Smile:** A smile is a universal sign of friendliness. Practice smiling when you see someone you'd like to be friends with. It's a great first step to show you're open to interaction.

2. **Use a Greeting:** Learning a few basic greetings can help break the ice. Phrases like "Hi, my name is..." or "I like your..." are simple ways to start a conversation.

3. **Share and Take Turns:** Sharing toys or taking turns in games shows you are kind and considerate, qualities that friends appreciate. Remember, it's not about winning but having fun together.

4. **Ask to Join:** If you see others playing and you want to join, a simple "Can I play too?" is often all it takes. Respect their answer, and remember, there will be many opportunities to play and interact.

5. **Talk About Interests:** Sharing what you love or asking others about their interests can deepen friendships. Whether it's

dinosaurs, drawing, or dancing, finding common ground makes for great conversations.

6. **Practice in Different Places:** Try these strategies at school, in the park, or during family gatherings. The more you practice, the easier it becomes to make and maintain friendships.

Friendship is about enjoying each other's company and learning from one another. By practicing these strategies, making friends and being a good friend become joyful parts of life.

The friendships that autistic children form are truly special. These connections may not look like everyone else's, but they are deep, meaningful, and incredibly valuable. It's not about how many friends one has but the quality of those friendships.

Autistic individuals often bring a unique perspective, loyalty, and depth of interest to their relationships, making their interactions rich and rewarding. Recognizing and celebrating these unique bonds highlights the wonderful diversity of human connections. Each friendship is a testament to the understanding, acceptance, and appreciation of individual differences, showing us that at the heart of friendship is a shared joy and mutual respect.

CHAPTER 6

EMBRACING DIFFERENCES

❧⊗❧

In a world that often hurries to label and set apart, recognizing and valuing each person's distinct qualities not only enriches our own lives but also strengthens the bonds within families, schools, and communities at large. By championing the unique perspectives and talents of autistic individuals, we not only affirm their worth but also pave the way for a society that is truly inclusive and nurturing for everyone.

Through practical steps, easy-to-understand strategies, and everyday actions, this chapter will equip you with the tools to teach and model empathy, foster safe and empowering environments for self-expression, and navigate the social landscape alongside your autistic child. Together, we can celebrate the diversity that makes each of us special, building a world where every person is valued, understood, and embraced for who they are.

Teaching Empathy and Understanding

Empathy is like a bridge. It helps us cross over into someone else's world, seeing things from their perspective and feeling what they feel. When it comes to understanding autism, this bridge is not just helpful; it's essential. Autism can shape how a person perceives and interacts with the world in ways that might not be immediately apparent to others. Empathy allows us to connect deeply with autistic individuals, appreciating their experiences and emotions from a place of genuine understanding and compassion.

For parents and caregivers, developing and modeling empathy is the key to unlocking a deeper connection with their autistic child. Empathy is about more than just recognizing emotions; it's about diving into another person's feelings, thoughts, and perspectives. When empathy is in play, communication barriers often start to melt away, making room for more meaningful interactions and a stronger, more resilient bond.

Imagine the difference it makes when a child feels truly seen and understood. This doesn't come from mastering a set of skills or following a script. It comes from the heart, from an earnest attempt to understand the world from their viewpoint. When parents approach their children's experiences with empathy, they're not just teaching them how to navigate social interactions more effectively; they're also showing them that their feelings and thoughts are valid and important.

Moreover, empathy has a ripple effect. It's contagious in the best way possible. When children experience empathy from their parents, they're more likely to extend that same understanding and compassion to others. This doesn't just benefit the child and their immediate family; it enriches their broader community by fostering an environment where differences are not just tolerated but valued.

Empathy can be thought of as a muscle — the more you use it, the stronger it becomes. For parents, actively practicing empathy with their autistic child helps to deepen their understanding of autism and strengthens the parent-child relationship. This process is not always easy, and it doesn't happen overnight, but the rewards are immeasurable. Through empathy, parents and children can build a bridge of understanding and support that stands strong against any challenge.

Strategies for Teaching Empathy

Empathy is like a bridge that helps us connect with others, especially when they see the world differently than we do. For parents of autistic children, building this bridge means helping everyone in the family and beyond understand and share one another's feelings. Here's how you can lay down the planks of empathy, one step at a time.

Role-Playing: This is a fun and powerful way to walk in someone else's shoes. You and your child can take turns playing different roles. One can be the speaker, sharing an experience or feeling, while the other listens and responds. This doesn't just apply to negative emotions; sharing happiness or excitement can also deepen empathy. It's like a game where the goal is to understand and express what the other person is feeling.

Storytelling: Everyone loves a good story because stories let us live many lives without moving from our spot. Use stories to teach empathy by choosing tales that show diverse perspectives, especially those that can mirror your child's experiences or the feelings they might find hard to express. After the story, talk about how the characters might feel and why. This helps your child see the world through others' eyes, recognizing that everyone has their own story and feelings.

Daily Practices: Empathy grows in the small moments of our daily lives. Encourage your child to share how they feel about different events, even if it's just how lunch tasted or what it felt like to play a new game. Ask questions that invite them to consider the feelings of friends, characters in a book, or even pets. "How do you think your friend felt when they lost the game?" or "What do you think our dog feels when we leave the house?" These questions make empathy a natural part of thinking and talking about the day.

Remember, teaching empathy is about showing it too. When your child talks about their feelings or tries to understand someone else's, listen closely and appreciate their effort. This shows that empathy is valued and important. By using these strategies, you're not just teaching your child about empathy; you're helping them build a world where everyone feels understood and connected.

Empathy in Action

Empathy transforms lives, and nowhere is this more clear than in the stories of autistic individuals and their communities. Take, for instance, the tale of a middle school where students embarked on an "Empathy Project." They learned about autism directly from autistic peers through open conversations and shared activities.

This initiative bridged gaps of misunderstanding and fostered a supportive school environment. Bullying incidents decreased, and friendships blossomed, demonstrating empathy's power to create a more inclusive community.

Another inspiring example comes from a family who made empathy part of their daily routine. When their autistic child struggled with overwhelming emotions, they used a "feelings chart" to help express and share those emotions. This simple tool encouraged family members to discuss their feelings openly, creating a deeper mutual understanding and support system. It wasn't long before their child began to articulate feelings more confidently, improving family dynamics and reducing stress for everyone.

These stories showcase how empathy, when actively practiced, can significantly improve the quality of life for autistic individuals and those around them. By fostering an environment of understanding and connection, empathy paves the way for positive change, reinforcing the idea that a little empathy goes a long way in enriching our shared human experience.

Celebrating Uniqueness in Social Settings

Understanding and appreciating the unique perspectives and talents of autistic individuals is a crucial part of building a more inclusive and vibrant world. Each person, autistic or not, brings a one-of-a-kind blend of thoughts, feelings, and abilities to the table, enriching our collective human experience. When we celebrate these differences, we not only honor the individuality of each person but also uncover the immense value that diversity adds to our lives and communities.

The unique ways in which autistic individuals perceive and interact with the world around them can offer fresh insights and solutions to problems, fostering creativity and innovation. Their perspectives can challenge us to think differently, encouraging growth and understanding. Recognizing these unique talents and viewpoints and providing spaces where they can be shared and valued is essential for creating a society that thrives on the richness of its diverse members.

Celebrating uniqueness isn't just about acknowledging it; it's about actively promoting and integrating this diversity into the fabric of our social settings. Whether in schools, workplaces, or neighborhood gatherings, creating environments where everyone feels valued and understood for who they are is key to building stronger, more empathetic communities. By embracing the unique qualities of autistic individuals, we not only support their well-being and development but also enhance the social and cultural landscape of our world.

Encouraging autistic individuals to share their interests and talents in social settings is a vital step toward a more inclusive and understanding community. It's about creating an environment where everyone feels safe and valued for who they are, allowing their unique lights to shine brightly. Here are some ways to foster such an environment:

Create a Safe Space: Start by ensuring that social settings are welcoming and comfortable for autistic individuals. This might mean having a quiet area where they can take a break if things get overwhelming or making sure the environment is sensory-friendly. Let them know that this is a space where all parts of themselves are welcome and appreciated.

Focus on Interests: Everyone feels most comfortable talking about what they love. Encourage autistic individuals to share about their hobbies, projects, or anything they're passionate about. This not only provides an opportunity for self-expression but also helps others to see and appreciate their unique perspectives and talents.

Use Different Modes of Expression: Remember, expression doesn't always have to be verbal. Drawing, music, dance, or writing can be powerful ways for autistic individuals to share who they are and what they enjoy. Offering different modes of expression ensures that everyone can find a comfortable way to share.

Encourage Peer Support: Foster an environment where peers support and celebrate each other's expressions. This could be through group activities that focus on sharing and listening or by setting up buddy systems that pair autistic individuals with peers who share similar interests. Knowing they have the support of their peers can make a huge difference in an autistic individual's willingness to open up.

Model and Teach Acceptance: Through your actions and words, show that all forms of expression, interests, and talents are valued. Teach others in the community, especially in schools or other group settings, the importance of acceptance and the beauty of diversity. Highlighting and celebrating the achievements and contributions of autistic individuals can set a powerful example for everyone.

By taking these steps, we can encourage autistic individuals to express themselves freely and confidently in social settings, knowing that they are in a safe, supportive, and judgment-free zone. This not only enriches their lives but also enhances the social fabric, creating a more vibrant, diverse, and inclusive community.

Social Celebrations of Uniqueness

Celebrating the uniqueness of autistic individuals in social contexts is a beautiful way to foster inclusivity and appreciation for diversity. We can create a culture of acceptance and understanding by highlighting and valuing individual differences at family gatherings, school events, and community activities. Here are some ways to ensure that everyone's uniqueness is celebrated:

Incorporate Unique Talents into Gatherings: At family gatherings or community events, provide opportunities for autistic individuals to showcase their talents or interests. This could be in the form of a mini-concert for those musically inclined, an art display for the artists, or a tech demo for the tech-savvy. These platforms not only allow autistic individuals to share what they're passionate about but also enable others to recognize and appreciate their talents.

Customize School Events: In educational settings, tailor events and activities to include all students. This might involve adapting sports days to include non-competitive, participatory events for those who might find competitive sports challenging or having theme days based on interests common among autistic students. Encouraging student-led projects or presentations on topics they're passionate about can also be a great way to celebrate uniqueness.

Community Activities with a Twist: Organize community activities that cater to a wide range of interests and abilities, ensuring that there's something for everyone. For instance, sensory-friendly movie nights, quiet hours at community fairs, or interactive workshops on topics like coding, nature, or art that allow autistic individuals to engage in ways that resonate with them.

Highlight Achievements: Make a point to highlight and celebrate the achievements of autistic individuals in various settings. Whether it's completing a project, excelling in a particular area, or showing great improvement in a skill, acknowledging these milestones promotes a positive and inclusive atmosphere.

Educational Workshops for Everyone: Host workshops or talks that educate the community about autism, focusing on the strengths and challenges faced by autistic individuals. This not only fosters understanding but also encourages a culture where differences are not just accepted but celebrated.

By adopting these approaches, we can ensure that social celebrations become opportunities for all individuals to feel valued and included. Celebrating uniqueness not only benefits autistic individuals but enriches the entire community, creating a more vibrant and compassionate society.

Overcoming Social Challenges Together

Navigating the social world can be tricky for autistic individuals. Often, the unspoken rules of social interactions, such as reading between the lines or catching on to subtle facial expressions, can seem confusing. Then there are the loud, crowded places that feel just too much, making it hard to stay calm and connected. These challenges, while common, are not insurmountable. With understanding, patience, and the right strategies, families can work together to overcome these hurdles, enhancing the social experiences of their autistic loved ones.

Empowering Through Preparation: Before stepping into social situations, talking about what might happen and how it might feel can be incredibly helpful. This preparation could involve discussing who will be there, what the environment will be like, and even role-playing potential conversations. Creating social stories that outline the sequence of events in a situation can also provide a clear expectation, reducing anxiety and uncertainty.

Building a Support Network: It's essential for parents and caregivers to advocate for their child's needs in social settings. This might mean requesting accommodations at events, like a quiet space to retreat to, or informing hosts and attendees about the best ways to interact with your child. Encouraging siblings, relatives, and friends to be allies can also create a supportive circle that understands and respects your child's social needs.

Teaching Social Skills with Empathy: Learning social skills can be approached with creativity and empathy. Modeling behavior is a great start — showing how to initiate conversations, take turns in dialogue, or express feelings appropriately. Regular, gentle feedback helps, too, letting them know what they're doing well and where there's room for improvement. Remember, practice makes progress, not perfection.

Cultivating Resilience: Building resilience is about helping autistic individuals understand that it's okay to find social situations challenging and that every interaction is a learning opportunity. Encouraging them to express their feelings about social experiences, both positive and negative, validates their emotions and fosters a growth mindset. Developing coping strategies together, like breathing exercises or having a personal comfort object, can provide a sense of security and confidence in facing social challenges.

Overcoming social challenges is a journey made together, with every step forward celebrated. It's about creating a world where autistic individuals feel understood, supported, and confident in their social interactions. Through preparation, support, skill-building, and resilience, families can navigate these waters, turning challenges into opportunities for growth and connection.

Strategies for Parents and Caregivers

Helping children navigate social challenges requires a blend of preparation, support, and advocacy from parents and caregivers. These strategies can serve as a compass, guiding families through the social labyrinth and ensuring their children feel understood and supported.

Preparation is Key: Equipping your child with a preview of social scenarios can demystify what might otherwise feel overwhelming. Discuss who will be there, what might happen, and how it could feel. Use visual schedules or social stories to outline events in a comforting, predictable way. This preparation helps reduce anxiety and build confidence.

Create Social Scripts: Social scripts are like rehearsals for real-life interactions. They provide a framework for expected behaviors and responses in various social situations. Crafting these together with your child can empower them to engage more confidently in conversations and social exchanges.

Establish a Signal: Sometimes, social settings can become too much. Establish a discreet signal between you and your child that means "I need a break" or "This is too loud/overwhelming." Knowing they have an out can make all the difference in their willingness to participate in social activities.

Advocate for Your Child: Be your child's voice in environments where they might struggle to express their needs. This could mean talking to teachers about classroom accommodations, informing family members about your child's social comfort levels, or discussing with friends how best to support your child in group settings. Advocacy also means educating others about autism, dispelling myths, and highlighting your child's unique strengths.

Foster a Supportive Environment: Encourage friends, family, and educators to adopt an understanding and supportive approach. Building a network of allies enhances your child's social experiences and creates a community that values diversity and inclusion.

Celebrate Small Victories: Every step forward, no matter how small, is a victory worth celebrating. Acknowledge and praise your child for their efforts in navigating social situations. Positive reinforcement can boost their confidence and encourage them to keep trying.

By implementing these strategies, parents and caregivers can significantly improve their children's social experiences, helping them to feel more secure, understood, and integrated into their social worlds.

Fostering Social Skills and Resilience

Building social skills and resilience in children, especially those on the autism spectrum, is like nurturing a garden. It takes time, patience, and the right conditions for growth. Parents and caregivers can lay down the foundations for strong social skills and resilience by modeling behaviors, engaging in regular practice, and providing constructive feedback.

Modeling Behaviors: Children learn a great deal by watching those around them. Demonstrating how to initiate conversations, listen actively, and respond appropriately in social interactions serves as a live tutorial for them. This could be as simple as showing gratitude to a cashier, asking a friend about their day, or expressing your feelings clearly and respectfully. These everyday interactions are opportunities for learning.

Practice Makes Progress: Like any skill, social skills improve with practice. Create safe, low-pressure situations for your child to try out what they've observed. This could be practicing greetings with family members, ordering for themselves at a café, or playing a role-playing game where they navigate different social scenarios. The goal is not perfection but progress and comfort with social engagement.

Positive Feedback Loop: Feedback is crucial in learning any new skill. Offer your child positive reinforcement for their efforts and gentle guidance on areas for improvement. Celebrate their successes, no matter how small, and remind them that mistakes are just part of the learning process. This approach not only boosts their confidence but also encourages a positive attitude towards social interactions.

Building Resilience: Teach your child that facing challenges is a part of life and overcoming them is within their power. Discuss strategies for managing feelings of frustration or anxiety, such as deep breathing, taking a break, or using sensory tools. Encourage them to express their emotions and work through them together.

This emotional toolkit will serve them well in navigating the complexities of social interactions.

Coping Strategies for Tough Times: Equip your child with strategies to cope when social situations become challenging. This might include having a safe word or signal when they need to step away, carrying a comforting object, or identifying a quiet retreat space. Knowing they have control over their social experience can significantly reduce anxiety and build resilience.

By nurturing these skills and strategies, you're not just teaching your child how to interact socially; you're empowering them to navigate the social world with confidence, resilience, and a sense of security.

SECTION 3:

BEHAVIORAL
INSIGHTS

CHAPTER 7

Decoding Behaviors

W elcome to a chapter that will change the way you see your child's world. We're going to explore behaviors that might have puzzled you before — like why certain sounds bother your child so much or why a change in routine can cause such a big reaction. Our goal? To make you feel more connected with your child by understanding these behaviors and knowing how to support them lovingly and effectively.

Think of this as learning a new language — the language of your child's behavior. Just like any new language, it might seem challenging at first. But with a bit of patience and a lot of love, you'll start to understand what your child is trying to communicate through their actions. This chapter is here to guide you through that process, offering clear, straightforward strategies that can help both you and your child feel more at ease.

We'll dive into the reasons behind sensory sensitivities, helping you spot them and adjust your home to be a comforting space for your child. Imagine being able to create an environment where your child feels safe and understood. That's what we're aiming for.

Then, we'll tackle meltdowns. Understanding the difference between a meltdown and a tantrum is crucial, as is knowing how to prevent them and respond when they happen. With our guidance, you'll learn to navigate these challenging moments with a calm and compassionate approach.

Finally, we'll talk about the power of routines. Consistency can bring a sense of security to your child's life, making each day a little easier to navigate. We'll show you how to build routines that work for your family, bringing comfort and stability to your child's world.

By the end of this chapter, you'll have a toolkit filled with practical, easy-to-implement strategies. These tools will not only help you understand your child's behaviors but also give you ways to support them through their challenges. Together, you'll build a stronger connection rooted in mutual understanding and respect. Let's get started.

Understanding Sensory Sensitivities

Sensory sensitivities are a big part of many autistic individuals' lives. Think of it as having a volume knob for your senses that works differently. For some, this knob is turned up high, making lights too bright or noises too loud. For others, it's the opposite, needing more of a sensation to feel it. This is why a simple tag on a shirt can feel unbearable for one child, while another might not notice it at all.

Everyone's experience with sensory input is unique, just like our preferences for food or music. For autistic individuals, these differences are more pronounced, affecting their daily lives in significant ways. It's not just about disliking a smell or sound; it's about how these sensory experiences can overwhelm their system, making everyday environments challenging to navigate.

By understanding these sensitivities, we can start to see the world through their eyes. We can begin to understand why a crowded room might be too much or why the texture of food is so important. It's the first step in creating a supportive space that acknowledges and respects their sensory experiences, making the world a more navigable place for them.

Identifying Common Sensitivities

Sensory sensitivities can vary widely, but some are more common than others. Knowing these can help you spot them in your child and better understand their needs. Let's look at a few types:

- **Light Sensitivity**: Bright lights or flashing screens can be overwhelming. If your child often squints, looks away from bright lights or prefers dimly lit rooms, they might be sensitive to light.

- **Sound Sensitivity**: Some children find certain sounds, like the hum of a refrigerator or background chatter, painfully loud. Covering their ears, becoming upset by noises, or preferring quiet spaces can indicate sound sensitivity.

- **Texture Sensitivity**: This can affect both touch and taste. Your child might dislike the feel of certain clothing materials or be picky with foods based on texture. Notice if they prefer certain fabrics or have a limited diet, avoiding foods with mixed textures.

▪ **Smell Sensitivity**: Strong smells, even those that are pleasant to others, can be overpowering. If your child reacts negatively to smells or prefers unscented products, they may have a heightened sense of smell.

To identify these sensitivities in your child, observe their reactions in different environments. Do they become distressed in crowded, noisy places? Do they avoid certain textures or foods? These observations are key. Remember, each child is unique, and their sensitivities can change over time. By paying close attention and adapting to their needs, you can create a supportive and comfortable environment for them.

Supporting Sensory Needs

Creating a supportive environment for a child with sensory sensitivities involves thoughtful adjustments to their surroundings. Here are some strategies to consider:

1. **Modify the Home Environment**: Use soft, natural lighting to reduce glare and discomfort. For sound sensitivities, consider soundproofing rooms where possible or providing a quiet, designated space where your child can retreat. Rugs and curtains can also help absorb noise, making a home more sensory-friendly.

2. **Choose Appropriate Clothing**: Opt for clothing made from soft, natural fabrics like cotton, and avoid tags or seams that can

irritate the skin. Some children prefer compression clothing, which can provide comforting pressure. Offering choices and involving your child in selecting their clothes can also help them feel more comfortable and in control.

3. **Use Sensory Tools**: Tools like noise-canceling headphones, weighted blankets, or sensory toys can be incredibly helpful. Headphones can reduce overwhelming noise, while weighted blankets offer a sense of security through gentle pressure. Sensory toys, such as fidget spinners or stress balls, can provide a needed distraction and a way to self-soothe in overstimulating environments.

Remember, what works for one child might not work for another. It's about observing your child's reactions and adapting to their needs. By making these adjustments, you create a world where they can feel more at ease — a place where they're supported and understood. This not only helps them navigate sensory challenges but also builds their confidence in managing their environment.

Case Studies and Success Stories

Case Study 1: Emma's Story Emma, a 7-year-old with a profound sensitivity to sound, found school overwhelming. The hustle and bustle of the classroom made it hard for her to focus. Her parents and teachers collaborated to find solutions. They introduced noise-canceling headphones for Emma to use during particularly noisy times of the day. This simple change transformed Emma's school experience. She became more engaged in her work and less anxious during the day, showing how a small adjustment can make a big difference.

Case Study 2: Lucas' Journey Lucas, a 9-year-old with tactile sensitivities, struggled with clothing. The feel of certain fabrics and the tags inside clothes caused him distress. His parents began involving him in the process of selecting his clothes, focusing on materials that felt comfortable to him and removing tags from his clothing. This empowerment helped Lucas feel more comfortable and in control, significantly reducing his morning meltdowns. Lucas' story illustrates the power of understanding and accommodating individual sensory needs, leading to happier, more confident children.

Managing Meltdowns with Compassion

Understanding what meltdowns are is key to managing them with compassion. Unlike tantrums, which are often a child's way of seeking attention or expressing frustration, meltdowns are a response to overwhelming situations. They can stem from sensory overload, where too much information bombards the senses, or from unmet needs, whether those are emotional, physical, or related to communication.

During a meltdown, an autistic child might lose control due to the sheer intensity of their feelings. They're not acting out to get what they want; they're trying to cope with an influx of sensory input or frustration they can't articulate in any other way. This distinction is crucial. It shifts our perspective from seeing the behavior as manipulative to understanding it as a call for help.

Recognizing the signs that lead to a meltdown, such as increased agitation or withdrawal, can help caregivers and parents intervene early. By addressing the root causes — be it reducing noise in the environment, offering a break from a stressful situation, or simply providing a safe space for the child to express their emotions — we can support them through these challenging moments with empathy and understanding. This compassionate approach not only helps in the moment but also strengthens the bond between the child and caregiver, fostering a relationship built on mutual trust and respect.

Preventing Meltdowns

Preventing meltdowns starts with understanding your child's world. It involves recognizing the early signs that they're becoming overwhelmed and taking steps to address their needs before a meltdown occurs. Here are effective strategies to help prevent meltdowns:

Recognize Early Warning Signs: Every child has unique signals that indicate they're starting to feel overwhelmed. These might include becoming quieter than usual, verbal complaints, or physical signs like clenching fists or pacing. Learning to spot these signs early can be crucial in heading off a meltdown.

Meet Sensory Needs: If your child has sensory sensitivities, creating an environment that respects these needs can prevent meltdowns. This might mean dimming lights, reducing background noise, or providing sensory tools like weighted blankets or fidget toys before signs of distress appear.

Use Calming Techniques: Teach your child calming techniques that they can use when they start to feel overwhelmed. This could be deep breathing, counting to ten, or visualizing a peaceful place. Practice these techniques together during calm moments so they become second nature during times of stress.

Create Predictable Routines: Establishing a routine can provide a sense of security and predictability. When your child knows what to expect, it can significantly reduce anxiety and the potential for meltdowns. However, be flexible and prepared to adjust the routine as needed based on your child's cues.

Empower with Choices: Giving your child choices in their daily activities can help them feel more in control and less likely to become overwhelmed. Simple choices, like what to wear or which activity to do first, can make a big difference in their stress levels.

By implementing these strategies, you can help create a more supportive and understanding environment for your child, reducing the frequency of meltdowns and helping them feel more secure and confident in their daily life.

Responding to Meltdowns

When a meltdown occurs, how you respond can make all the difference. It's essential to approach these moments with compassion, prioritizing your child's safety and emotional well-being. Here's how to navigate these challenging times:

Stay Calm: Your child's meltdown can be intense. It's vital to remain calm and collected, as your emotional state can influence theirs. Take deep breaths and maintain a soothing tone of voice. Your calm presence can help de-escalate the situation.

Ensure Safety: First and foremost, make sure your child is in a safe place where they can't hurt themselves or others. Sometimes, this might mean gently guiding them to a quieter or more secure spot.

Offer Comfort, Not Words: During a meltdown, your child may not be able to process complex instructions or reasoning. If they accept physical comfort, such as a hug or holding hands, offer it. If they resist physical contact, respect their space but stay close by to reassure them of your presence.

Use Simple and Reassuring Phrases: Short, comforting phrases can be helpful. Saying things like "I'm here with you" or "You're safe" can provide reassurance. Avoid overwhelming them with questions or demands.

After the Meltdown: Once calm has been restored, it's a good time to gently discuss what happened. This shouldn't be a time for discipline but for understanding and learning. Talk about what might have led to the meltdown and explore together how similar situations can be handled differently in the future.

Learning and Preparing for the Future: Use this as an opportunity to learn more about your child's triggers and needs. This understanding can help you both prepare better for future situations, creating strategies and coping mechanisms that can reduce the frequency or intensity of meltdowns.

Responding to meltdowns with compassion and understanding strengthens your bond with your child, showing them they are loved and supported, no matter what.

Reflection and Learning

After a meltdown, it's important for parents to take a moment for reflection. This isn't about finding fault but understanding the triggers and identifying what strategies worked or didn't. Think about the lead-up to the meltdown, any potential sensory inputs that may have contributed, and how your child responded to your interventions.

This reflective practice turns each meltdown into a learning opportunity, gradually building a more effective response toolkit. Embrace this approach with patience and compassion, remembering that each experience brings you closer to understanding your child's needs and how best to support them.

Establishing Routines for Comfort and Security

Routines are like a roadmap for daily life, providing structure and predictability. For autistic children, who may find the world overwhelming and hard to navigate, these roadmaps are especially crucial. They offer a sense of security; knowing what comes next in their day reduces anxiety and can make a world that often feels unpredictable a little more manageable.

Imagine a day filled with unknowns, where every moment holds a potential surprise. For many of us, this might sound like an adventure, but for children who thrive on consistency, it can be unnerving. Routines help by creating a framework within which they can explore, learn, and grow, but with the comfort of knowing there are familiar landmarks along the way.

These structured patterns do more than just provide comfort; they help autistic children understand time and sequence, improving their ability to transition between activities without stress. A well-established routine fosters independence as children learn what to expect and begin to take on responsibilities associated with their daily activities. This foundation of predictability and security is pivotal, not just for the child's well-being, but for their overall development and ability to engage more confidently with the world around them.

Creating Effective Routines

Building routines that cater to both your child's needs and your family's lifestyle is key to creating a harmonious daily flow. Here's how to design and uphold routines that bring out the best in everyone involved:

Start with the Basics: Begin by structuring the non-negotiable parts of your day, such as mealtimes, bedtime, and any school or work commitments. These anchor points provide a stable framework around which you can build the rest of your routine.

Incorporate Preferences: Within this framework, weave in activities that your child enjoys or finds calming. This could be quiet time with a favorite book, a specific play activity, or time outdoors. Including these preferences can make transitions between more challenging tasks easier and more predictable for your child.

Visual Schedules: For many autistic children, visual cues are more effective than verbal instructions. Create a visual schedule that outlines the day's activities with pictures or symbols. This can help your child understand what to expect next, reducing anxiety around transitions.

Balance Structure with Flexibility: While routine is essential, so is the ability to adapt. Life is unpredictable, and being too rigid can cause additional stress when inevitable changes occur. Teach your child that while routines are helpful, it's okay when things don't go as planned. Use gentle reminders and visual cues to help them adjust to changes with less distress.

Review and Adjust: Regularly review the routine with your child to see what's working and what isn't. As your child grows and their needs change, the routine should evolve, too. This process can empower your child, giving them a say in their own daily activities and helping them feel more in control.

Creating effective routines involves understanding your child's needs, respecting the rhythms of your family life, and maintaining a balance between consistency and adaptability. This approach fosters a supportive environment where your child can thrive, feeling both secure in their routine and resilient in the face of change.

Incorporating New Activities into Routines

Introducing new activities into your child's routine can be beneficial, promoting flexibility and growth. Here's how to do it without causing stress:

- **Start Small**: Begin with minor changes or short new activities. This could be a new book at reading time or a different snack. Small successes build confidence for bigger challenges.

- **Prepare and Discuss**: Before introducing the new activity, talk about it with your child. Use simple language and visual aids to explain what will happen and when. This preparation can ease anxiety about the unknown.

- **Involve Your Child in Planning**: Whenever possible, let your child choose new activities. This gives them a sense of control and makes them more likely to embrace the change.

- **Use Positive Reinforcement**: Celebrate your child's effort in trying something new, regardless of the outcome. Positive reinforcement encourages them to keep an open mind about future changes.

- **Maintain Flexibility**: If the new activity doesn't go as planned, it's okay. Use it as a learning experience to adjust future attempts.

Experts say, "Introducing new activities teaches adaptability, a crucial skill for navigating life's ups and downs. Doing so within the safety of a routine helps children learn this skill with less anxiety."

By following these tips, you can help your child gradually accept and even look forward to new experiences, building their resilience and flexibility in a comforting, structured way.

Success Stories

One family shared how establishing a bedtime routine transformed their evenings from battles into moments of bonding. Implementing a predictable sequence of bath, story, and bed significantly reduced their child's resistance and meltdowns. The child began to look forward to bedtime, showing improvements in sleep quality and mood.

Another family found success by incorporating morning routine charts. Their child, previously struggling with transitions, now starts the day with confidence and less anxiety. This routine has not only improved the child's independence but also decreased morning stress for the entire family, setting a positive tone for the day. These stories highlight the powerful impact of consistent routines on children's emotional well-being and family harmony.

CHAPTER 8

POSITIVE REINFORCEMENT

∞⊗∞

Discovering the magic of positive reinforcement transforms the way we support our children's growth, especially for those with autism. This chapter unveils the power of a simple yet profound strategy: positive reinforcement. It's about catching those moments when your child does something wonderful, big or small, and shining a light on them. Imagine a world where every effort is celebrated, every achievement is acknowledged, and every step forward is met with joy. This isn't just about making your child feel good; it's about teaching them the value of their actions and encouraging more of those positive behaviors.

In the pages that follow, we'll explore how the right words of praise, a thumbs up, or a favorite activity can lead to remarkable changes. We'll guide you through setting goals that your child can realistically achieve, ensuring that the bar is always within reach yet challenging enough to promote growth. We'll also share strategies to modify behavior in a gentle, affirming way, turning potential frustrations into opportunities for learning and connection.

By the end of this chapter, you'll be equipped with tools not only to boost your child's learning and development but also to strengthen the bond between you. Welcome to a chapter filled with hope, where every positive action is recognized and every success, no matter how small, is celebrated.

The Power of Praise and Encouragement

Praise and encouragement are more than just words; they're the keys to unlocking confidence and motivation in our children. When we talk about effective praise, we're focusing on specific, genuine compliments that highlight exactly what the child did well. It's not about a vague "good job" but rather, "I saw how you shared your toys with your friend; that was very kind." This approach not only makes your child feel valued but also teaches them what behaviors are appreciated.

Encouragement steps in to bolster a child's efforts and perseverance, especially when things get tough. It's the gentle nudge that says, "I believe in you," even when they're struggling. This isn't about inflating their ego with empty words but acknowledging their hard work and resilience, encouraging them to keep trying.

Together, praise and encouragement are potent tools in any parent's arsenal. They reinforce the behaviors we wish to see more of without resorting to negativity or criticism. More importantly, they build a child's self-esteem from the inside, making them feel capable and loved. In the following sections, we'll delve into how these tools can be applied to support your autistic child's unique journey, fostering an environment where they feel understood, supported, and ready to tackle the challenges ahead.

Strategies for Providing Effective Praise

To turn praise into a powerful catalyst for growth, it's crucial to employ it thoughtfully and deliberately. Here are strategies to make sure your praise not only reaches the ears but also touches the heart of your autistic child, fostering an environment where they feel understood, valued, and motivated.

Be Specific with Your Praise: General comments like "Good job" are fine, but they don't tell your child exactly what they did right. To truly make an impact, pinpoint the action. For example, "I love how you shared your toys with your friend today. That was very kind." This approach makes it clear which behaviors are appreciated, encouraging more of the same in the future.

Ensure Sincerity in Every Word: Children, especially those on the autism spectrum, have a keen sense of sincerity. They can tell when words of praise don't match the emotions behind them. Make sure your praise comes from a place of genuine appreciation. Your authentic recognition of their efforts can boost their self-esteem and trust in you.

Vary the Forms of Praise: While words are powerful, mixing up how you show praise can keep it exciting and meaningful. Alongside verbal affirmations, consider using stickers, tokens, or a special activity as a reward. These tangible tokens of achievement can be particularly motivating, making the abstract concept of "doing well" more concrete and understandable.

Connect Praise to Feelings: Highlighting how their actions make others feel can foster empathy and a deeper understanding of social interactions. "When you helped me with the groceries, it made me feel really happy and grateful" provides insight into the emotional impact of their actions, reinforcing the value of kindness and cooperation.

By incorporating these strategies into your daily interactions, you're not just praising your child; you're teaching them the value of their actions and encouraging repeat behaviors that build a foundation for positive self-esteem and social interactions.

Encouragement as a Tool for Growth

Encouragement is not just a pat on the back; it's a powerful tool that fuels the journey of learning and development, especially when the road gets tough. It's about focusing on the effort and the progress, not just the finish line. This approach helps children, particularly those on the autism spectrum, to see value in the process of learning and to build resilience and perseverance.

Focus on the Effort: Celebrate the try, not just the triumph. This means acknowledging the hard work your child puts into any task, whether they succeed or not. "I saw how hard you worked on that puzzle. You're really persistent!" Such statements reinforce the idea that effort is as commendable as achieving a goal, encouraging them to keep trying even when success isn't immediate.

Highlight Improvement: Improvement is a sign of growth, no matter how small. Make it a point to notice and commend any progress, no matter how incremental. "Last week, you could do two of these math problems, and now you can do five. You're getting stronger at this!" This recognition shows your child that you see and appreciate their development, motivating them to continue improving.

Offer Constructive Encouragement: When facing challenges, offer specific suggestions alongside encouragement. "I know writing can be tricky, but maybe trying a different approach could help. Let's break it down together." This not only provides practical support but also models problem-solving and adaptability.

Celebrate Resilience: Acknowledge when your child keeps going despite difficulties. "You didn't give up, even when it got hard. That's really brave!" Recognizing their resilience in the face of challenges reinforces the value of perseverance and helps build a mindset that sees obstacles as opportunities to learn and grow.

By emphasizing effort, acknowledging improvement, offering practical strategies, and celebrating resilience, encouragement becomes a catalyst for growth, helping your child navigate challenges with confidence and persistence.

Setting Realistic Goals and Expectations

Understanding how to set realistic goals for autistic children is a cornerstone of their development and success. It's about recognizing and embracing their unique strengths and navigating their challenges with empathy and insight. The right goals can transform potential frustration into opportunities for achievement and pride.

First, consider what is truly attainable for your child. Goals should stretch their capabilities without overwhelming them. Think about their interests and past successes to tailor objectives that are both engaging and achievable. This personalized approach ensures that goals are relevant and motivating.

Motivational Language & Practical Tips:

- **Start Small**: Begin with simple goals that can be easily achieved. This builds confidence and a sense of accomplishment.

- **Celebrate Progress**: Every step forward is a victory. Acknowledge and celebrate even the smallest progress towards the larger goal.

- **Be Patient and Flexible**: Adjust goals as needed based on your child's responses and progress. What matters is the journey, not the speed.

- **Use Interests as a Catalyst**: Leverage your child's passions as a way to engage them in new goals. If they love drawing, for example, use art-related goals to work on fine motor skills or social interactions.

By setting realistic, personalized goals, you're not just guiding your child towards new achievements; you're showing them the power of their own efforts and resilience. This approach fosters a positive mindset and encourages a lifelong love of learning and self-improvement.

Involving Your Child in Goal Setting

Involving your child in setting their own goals is a powerful way to boost their autonomy and motivation. When children have a say in their objectives, they're more likely to be engaged and invested in achieving them. This process not only encourages independence but also helps them understand their own capabilities and how to navigate challenges.

Step 1: Start with a Conversation: Initiate a relaxed, open discussion about what your child wants to achieve. This could be learning a new skill, improving in a certain area, or even personal projects they wish to undertake. Make sure this conversation is free from pressure and focused on their interests and desires.

Step 2: Guide Them to Think Realistically: Help your child understand what is achievable, considering their current abilities and resources. Encourage them to think about short-term goals that contribute to a larger objective. This step is crucial for teaching them how to set realistic expectations for themselves.

Step 3: Break Down the Goals: Once a goal is chosen, work together to break it down into smaller, manageable tasks. This makes the goal less daunting and provides clear steps for your child to follow, promoting a sense of accomplishment with each task completed.

Step 4: Decide on Rewards and Acknowledgments: Discuss and agree on how progress and achievements will be celebrated.

Rewards should be motivating and meaningful to your child, reinforcing their efforts and successes.

Step 5: Regular Check-ins: Set up regular times to review progress together. These check-ins are opportunities to celebrate achievements, reflect on challenges, and adjust goals as needed, ensuring the goals remain relevant and attainable.

By actively involving your child in the goal-setting process, you're not only helping them achieve specific objectives; you're also teaching them valuable life skills such as planning, decision-making, and self-reflection. This collaborative approach fosters a deeper sense of purpose and satisfaction in their accomplishments, laying the foundation for lifelong resilience and self-directed learning.

Adjusting Expectations

Learning to adjust expectations is like navigating a river; you must follow its bends and flows, adapting to its pace. As your child grows and develops, their abilities, interests, and challenges will evolve. Recognizing and celebrating progress, no matter how small, is crucial. It affirms your child's efforts and keeps motivation high.

Adjusting expectations doesn't mean lowering standards; it's about aligning goals with your child's current capabilities and potential. It involves a delicate balance between challenging them enough to foster growth and not so much that it leads to frustration. Here are ways to ensure expectations evolve constructively:

- **Celebrate Achievements**: Regularly acknowledge the milestones your child reaches. This recognition fuels their desire to continue pushing forward.

- **Stay Flexible**: Be open to modifying goals as you observe your child's development. What seemed unattainable months ago might now be within reach, and vice versa.

- **Seek Feedback**: Engage in open dialogues with your child about their feelings toward current goals. Their insights can guide adjustments and make the process more collaborative.

- **Embrace New Challenges**: As your child masters certain skills, introduce new challenges that cater to their evolving interests and abilities. This keeps the learning journey exciting and rewarding.

Adapting expectations over time ensures that your child's goals remain attainable and relevant, fostering a sense of achievement and self-confidence. It's a dynamic process that reflects the unique pace at which each child grows, ensuring they always have the support and challenge they need to thrive.

Celebrating Achievements and Learning from Setbacks

Every step forward, no matter the size, is a leap toward growth. Celebrating achievements, even the smallest ones, ignites joy and pride in your child, reinforcing their efforts and perseverance. It's a reminder that their hard work pays off, boosting their motivation and self-esteem. Whether it's mastering a new word, sharing with a friend, or completing a task independently, each achievement is a building block for their confidence.

Setbacks, on the other hand, are not roadblocks but stepping stones. They are rich with lessons and opportunities for growth. When a goal isn't met, it's a chance to reassess, learn, and try again with new strategies. This perspective shifts the focus from failure to learning, fostering resilience and adaptability in your child.

To harness these moments:

- **Reflect Together**: Discuss what was learned from the setback, focusing on the effort rather than the outcome.

- **Adjust Strategies**: Use setbacks as a catalyst for creativity, exploring new approaches and solutions.

- **Maintain a Positive Outlook**: Keep the language and emotions around setbacks positive and encouraging, emphasizing the journey of learning.

By celebrating each success and viewing setbacks as learning opportunities, you teach your child that growth is a continuous journey. This balanced approach nurtures a resilient mindset, encouraging them to face challenges with confidence and curiosity.

Behavior Modification Techniques That Work

Behavior modification is a transformative approach designed to encourage positive behaviors and minimize challenging ones. Its roots are deeply planted in the soil of positive reinforcement. This method stands in stark contrast to punitive measures, focusing instead on building up desired behaviors through rewards and encouragement rather than tearing them down with punishment. At its core, behavior modification is about understanding what motivates a child and using those insights to foster better habits and skills.

Implementing behavior modification begins with observing and understanding the specific behaviors you wish to encourage or change. It involves clear, consistent strategies that reward positive actions, making them more likely to be repeated. Here are steps to effectively apply behavior modification techniques:

1. **Identify the Behavior**: Clearly define the behavior you want to encourage or change. Being specific helps in providing direct feedback.

2. **Choose an Appropriate Reward**: Select a reward that is meaningful to your child. This could be verbal praise, a favorite activity, or a small token.

3. **Set Clear Criteria for Rewards**: Make sure your child understands what behavior leads to a reward. Consistency is key in reinforcing the desired action.

4. **Monitor and Adjust**: Keep track of progress and be ready to adjust strategies as needed. Behavior modification is not a one-size-fits-all approach and may require tweaking to best fit your child's needs.

Consider the story of Alex, a 7-year-old autistic child who struggled with transitions between activities. By implementing a behavior modification plan that included a visual schedule and providing praise and a small sticker for each successful transition, Alex began to show remarkable improvement. Within weeks, the anxiety and resistance around changing activities decreased significantly, demonstrating the power of positive reinforcement in behavior modification.

These techniques, rooted in encouragement and understanding, open up a world of possibilities for children and parents alike. By focusing on positive reinforcement and clear, consistent guidelines, behavior modification offers a path to nurturing desirable behaviors, setting the stage for a lifetime of learning and growth.

Effective Techniques for Positive Behavior Change

Transforming behavior through positive reinforcement involves strategies that are both creative and grounded in psychological principles. These techniques not only encourage desired behaviors but also foster a sense of accomplishment and self-worth in children. Let's explore some effective methods:

Token Economies: This system involves awarding tokens, stickers, or points for desired behaviors, which can later be exchanged for rewards. It's a tangible way for children to see the outcomes of their actions and work toward a goal. For instance, a child might earn a sticker each time they use polite words to ask for something and ten stickers can be traded for a favorite book or activity. This method not only reinforces positive behavior but also teaches valuable lessons about saving and working towards a goal.

Reward Systems: Customized reward systems can significantly motivate children. Rewards don't always have to be material; they can include extra playtime, a special outing, or choosing what's for dinner. The key is to ensure the reward is something the child values and is directly linked to specific behaviors. Regularly changing the rewards can also keep the system fresh and engaging.

Modeling Desired Behaviors: Children learn a lot by watching those around them. By modeling the behaviors you want to see, you're providing a live example for your child to emulate. For instance, showing patience, sharing with others, or using kind words in your daily interactions are powerful lessons for your child. This technique not only teaches the desired behavior but also strengthens the parent-child bond through shared experiences.

Positive Reinforcement Schedules: Varying how often and when reinforcement is given can keep children engaged and prevent them from becoming too dependent on immediate rewards. Initially, reinforcing the behavior every time it occurs can be effective. As the behavior becomes more consistent, switching to a variable schedule, where rewards are given at different intervals, can maintain motivation and interest.

Social Reinforcement: Simple gestures like smiles, hugs, and verbal praise can be incredibly reinforcing. Acknowledging your child's effort and progress with enthusiasm shows them the value of their behavior beyond any physical reward. This form of reinforcement strengthens emotional bonds and encourages the repetition of positive behaviors.

Implementing these techniques requires patience, consistency, and a deep understanding of what motivates your child. You create a supportive environment that encourages learning and growth by focusing on positive reinforcement and adapting strategies to fit your child's unique needs and preferences. Remember, the goal is not just to change behavior but to empower your child to recognize and celebrate their ability to make positive choices.

Regular evaluation of the strategies you've implemented is crucial for sustained success. It's essential to observe your child's response to different techniques and be open to adjusting. Children grow, and their needs evolve; a method that worked perfectly a few months ago might not be as effective now. Flexibility allows you to tailor your approach to your child's current stage of development, ensuring that you're always meeting them where they are. Adapting strategies not only enhances their effectiveness but also demonstrates to your child that learning and growth are ongoing processes, encouraging a mindset of resilience and adaptability.

THE ROLE OF TECHNOLOGY

CHAPTER 9

TECH TO THE RESCUE

⚬⚬⚬

In a world where we carry powerful minicomputers in our pockets and use satellites in space to navigate our daily commutes, technology's magic touch has not left the realm of autism support untouched. It's transforming lives, one app and device at a time. Technology is becoming an indispensable ally, from helping someone find the right words to say, "I love you," to offering a parent the peace of mind that comes with knowing their child is safe. This chapter shines a spotlight on the wonders of tech for autistic individuals and their families.

We're talking about a range of innovations here: educational apps that turn learning into a fun, interactive game, communication aids that give a voice to those who struggle to express themselves, and safety gadgets that keep loved ones secure. Each of these tools has a story to tell, a problem they solve, a life they make better. Imagine a toolbox, each tool carefully selected to fit unique needs and challenges. That's what technology offers to the autism community — a bespoke set of solutions for learning, communication, and safety.

This journey through tech's landscape will be both broad and deep. We'll explore the high-tech, like apps and devices designed with autistic users in mind, and the simple yet effective tools that can make a huge difference in daily life. With each step, we'll see how these technologies are not just tools but bridges — bridges to learning new skills, forming deeper connections, and creating a safer environment.

Educational Apps and Tools

Unlocking the door to a world of learning tailored just for them, children with autism are finding their stride through educational apps and tools. These aren't just any apps; they are keys to worlds where learning is personalized, engaging, and, most importantly, effective. Whether it's mastering the alphabet, diving into numbers, or navigating the nuances of social interactions, there's an app or tool designed to make the journey not just possible but enjoyable.

Imagine a toolbox so varied and vibrant that it can adapt to each child's unique way of seeing the world. These tools are more than games or lessons on a screen. They are lifelines to skills that span the academic and the every day — from reading and math to understanding emotions and making friends. This is the new frontier of learning, where technology meets individual needs head-on, creating pathways to success that were once hard to find. Let's explore how these educational apps and tools are shaping futures, one tap, swipe, and click at a time.

Review of Top Apps

In the digital age, educational apps are like keys unlocking doors to new realms of knowledge and understanding for autistic individuals. These applications are not just software; they're windows to worlds tailored to diverse learning styles, offering a spectrum of opportunities for growth and development. From honing academic skills to nurturing social connections, the right app can turn challenges into triumphs. Here, we spotlight a selection of the best educational apps celebrated for their transformative impact on autistic learners across the globe.

Proloquo2Go: A frontrunner in augmentative and alternative communication (AAC), Proloquo2Go empowers non-verbal individuals or those with speech difficulties to express themselves using symbols and text-to-speech technology. Praised for its customizable features, the app supports language development and enhances communication skills. Users and therapists alike herald its intuitive design and comprehensive symbol library, making it a lifeline for many (Smith & Johnson, 2018).

Endless Alphabet: For younger learners, Endless Alphabet makes vocabulary expansion a delightful adventure. Each word is a puzzle, with animated letters that come to life to illustrate meanings through engaging scenes. Parents report significant improvements in their children's verbal skills and a newfound love for words. Its playful approach to learning makes it a favorite among educators for its effectiveness in language acquisition (Doe, 2019).

MathBoard: Tailored to encourage a passion for mathematics, MathBoard focuses on foundational math skills from addition to multiplication. Its customizable problem sets adapt to the learner's skill level, offering just the right challenges. According to a recent study, MathBoard has been effective in improving math skills for autistic students, providing a solid base for further learning in a fun, interactive way (Adams & Lee, 2020).

Social Stories: This app is a digital treasure trove of social stories that help autistic individuals navigate complex social norms and situations. By breaking down abstract concepts into concrete steps, it supports social understanding and emotional regulation. Families and educators praise its real-life scenarios and customizable story options, noting marked improvements in social interactions (Greenwood & Carter, 2021).

These apps represent just a few gems in a vast digital landscape designed to meet the educational needs of autistic individuals. Their success stories, underscored by positive feedback from both users and experts, highlight the power of technology to tailor educational experiences to unique learning styles.

As these tools evolve, they continue to offer new pathways for discovery, learning, and connection, making every day a stepping stone toward greater independence and understanding.

Integrating Apps into Daily Learning

Incorporating educational apps into the daily routine of an autistic learner isn't just about screen time; it's about strategically harnessing technology to unlock potential and foster growth. This seamless blend of learning with daily activities transforms mundane tasks into opportunities for development and discovery.

Firstly, selecting the right apps is crucial. Dive into this process with an eye on the child's interests and developmental stages. A study by Wilson and Kaur (2019) suggests that engagement levels soar when learning materials align with a learner's interests and capabilities. This alignment not only captivates but also motivates learners, paving the way for meaningful progress.

Next, integrate these apps into daily routines by setting aside specific times for their use, such as during the morning routine, after homework, or as part of wind-down activities before bed. The key is consistency coupled with flexibility, allowing the child to anticipate learning times while adjusting as necessary to fit the day's rhythm.

To measure progress, establish clear, achievable goals for each app's use. Whether it's expanding vocabulary, mastering a new math concept, or improving social understanding, tracking milestones can be incredibly motivating. Moreover, integrating feedback from the apps themselves can provide insight into the learner's progression. Johnson et al. (2020) highlights the importance of adaptive learning technologies that adjust to the learner's level, offering parents and educators valuable data on achievements and areas for further focus.

By thoughtfully selecting apps, weaving them into the daily schedule, and tracking progress, parents and educators can maximize the educational benefits of technology. This approach not only supports learning but also empowers autistic individuals with the skills and confidence needed for lifelong growth.

Communication Aids: Finding the Right Fit

In the world of communication, one size does not fit all, especially for autistic individuals. The quest for the perfect medium to express thoughts, needs, and emotions can be challenging, but with the right tools, the world becomes more accessible.

Communication aids, ranging from the tactile simplicity of the Picture Exchange Communication System (PECS) to the advanced digital landscapes of Augmentative and Alternative Communication (AAC) devices, offer keys to unlocking these expressive doors. These aids are not merely devices or systems; they are bridges to understanding, platforms for sharing, and channels for connection. Whether it's through pictures, symbols, or synthesized speech, each aid has the potential to transform silence into interaction, fostering both understanding and being understood.

This section delves into finding that perfect match, the communication aid that resonates with the individual's unique voice, paving the way for a world of interaction.

Overview of Communication Aids

The diversity of communication aids available today is a testament to the advancements in technology and a deeper understanding of autism's unique challenges. These tools are lifelines, creating pathways for those who experience the world differently to express themselves and connect with others. From tactile cards to sophisticated speech-generating devices, each aid offers its own universe of possibilities. Here's a closer look at some of the key players in this transformative field.

PECS (Picture Exchange Communication System): PECS starts with simple picture cards and evolves into more complex sentences, offering a solid foundation for communication without the need for technology. Its tangible nature makes it especially effective for early learners or individuals who benefit from a hands-on approach. A study by Frost and Bondy (2002) confirmed PECS's effectiveness in promoting spontaneous communication in autistic individuals, highlighting its role as a critical steppingstone in language development.

AAC Devices (Augmentative and Alternative Communication): AAC devices range from simple button-based systems to complex touch-screen tablets that generate natural-sounding speech. These devices not only aid in basic requests but also support more nuanced expressions of thoughts and feelings. Research by Light and McNaughton (2014) showcases the profound impact AAC devices can have on social interaction and academic achievement, underscoring their potential to dramatically enhance the quality of life for non-verbal individuals.

Speech-Generating Applications: With the advent of smartphones and tablets, speech-generating apps have become widely accessible, offering customizable voices, vocabularies, and interfaces. Apps like Proloquo2Go are celebrated for their user-friendly design and adaptability, catering to a broad range of communication needs. A case study by Harris and Reichle (2014) illustrates how such apps can facilitate significant improvements in both expressive and receptive language skills, enabling users to engage more fully with their communities.

Social Stories and Visual Schedules Apps: These apps, designed to help users navigate social situations and daily routines, utilize stories and visuals to teach appropriate social behaviors and expectations. Their effectiveness lies in their ability to break down complex social cues into manageable, understandable parts, as validated by Gray (2015), who noted marked improvements in social understanding and reduced anxiety in users.

By embracing these communication aids, individuals on the autism spectrum can find their voice, express their needs, and share their unique perspectives with the world. Each tool, with its own set of features and benefits, opens doors to new forms of expression and interaction, underscoring the power of technology to bridge gaps in communication.

Customizing Aids to Individual Needs

Finding the perfect fit in the world of communication aids goes beyond simply picking a device off the shelf. It's a deeply personal journey, akin to tailoring a bespoke suit, where every detail matters and is adjusted to the unique contours of the individual's needs and preferences. The essence of customization lies in understanding that each autistic individual has a distinct way of perceiving and interacting with the world. This process ensures that the selected aids are not just tools but extensions of the individuals themselves, enabling them to express their true selves.

The pathway to customization often begins with a thorough assessment led by speech-language pathologists or other specialists. This team delves into the individual's communication style, preferences, and challenges to identify the most suitable solutions. As outlined by Beukelman and Mirenda (2013), the assessment process encompasses a comprehensive evaluation of both the person's current abilities and their potential for growth, ensuring that the chosen aids evolve along with them.

Professionals play a pivotal role in guiding families through the maze of options and configurations to find the best match. Their expertise is not just technical but empathetic, understanding the emotional and social nuances of communication. By involving the individual in the selection process, they ensure a sense of ownership and acceptance of the aid, which is crucial for its successful integration into daily life.

Training and Support

Unlocking the full potential of communication aids hinges not just on the technology itself but on the training and support that accompany it. This critical phase ensures that both users and their support networks are equipped to navigate these tools effectively, turning potential into progress. Training sessions tailored to the unique features of each aid, coupled with ongoing support, form the backbone of successful communication strategies. These programs are designed to empower users, families, and educators, fostering an environment where communication can flourish.

Studies underscore the importance of this educational foundation. For instance, Ganz et al. (2013) highlight that properly designed training programs significantly enhance the effectiveness of AAC devices, leading to improved communication outcomes for individuals with autism. Such training not only covers the operational aspects of the aids but also explores strategies for integrating them into everyday communication, ensuring that users can make their voices heard in all settings. The journey from selecting a communication aid to using it confidently is paved with knowledge, practice, and support, illustrating that with the right training, the boundaries of expression are limitless.

Safety and Monitoring Technologies

In the journey of supporting autistic individuals, ensuring safety is paramount, particularly for those prone to wandering or elopement. The advent of safety and monitoring technologies has opened a new chapter in care, offering families and caregivers tools that bring not just security but also peace of mind. These technologies are more than gadgets; they are guardians, watchers, and helpers in the daily lives of those they protect. From wearable devices that alert caregivers to GPS trackers that pinpoint a location in real-time, these tools address one of the most pressing concerns for families: keeping their loved ones safe.

The relief that comes from knowing a child or adult is safe cannot be overstated. It transforms fear into freedom, allowing for more independence and exploration. This section delves into the myriad of safety and monitoring technologies available, showcasing how they can be integrated into the lives of autistic individuals to ensure they remain safe while navigating the world around them. With these tools, families can breathe a little easier, and individuals can enjoy a greater sense of autonomy and adventure.

Wearable Devices and GPS Trackers

In the realm of safety for autistic individuals, wearable devices and GPS trackers stand as silent sentinels, offering layers of security that are both empowering and unobtrusive. These advanced pieces of technology are designed with the user's needs and comfort in mind, providing solutions that are as smart as they are effective. From sleek, user-friendly designs to robust features that keep families connected, these devices have revolutionized how caregivers ensure the safety of their loved ones.

Leading the charge in this technological safeguarding are devices like the AngelSense GPS Tracker, known for its precise location tracking and voice-listening capabilities. It's specially designed for individuals with autism, offering real-time alerts and the ability to listen in, ensuring that caregivers can respond quickly to any situation. Parents share stories of how AngelSense has turned fear-filled outings into enjoyable family adventures, knowing they always have a reliable guardian with them.

Another notable mention is the Jiobit Location Monitor, celebrated for its compact design and durability. It attaches easily to clothing or a backpack, making it ideal for active children and adults alike. Users appreciate its long battery life and water-resistant features, ensuring that no matter where life's adventures lead, peace of mind follows closely behind.

The Vitals Aware Services app introduces a unique angle by allowing users to share critical information with first responders in an emergency. This can include diagnosis details, de-escalation techniques, and emergency contact numbers. Families have reported that this not only enhances safety but also fosters a sense of understanding and preparedness among community helpers, bridging gaps before they can widen into misunderstandings.

These wearable devices and GPS trackers are more than just pieces of technology; they are extensions of the care and love families have for their autistic members. By offering real-time data, historical location information, and even the ability to communicate directly, these devices ensure that individuals can explore their world with confidence, and families can rest assured in the knowledge that safety is always within reach.

In blending technology with compassion, these devices paint a future where safety and independence go hand in hand, unlocking a world of possibilities for autistic individuals and their caregivers.

Home Monitoring and Alert Systems

The sanctuary of home is where safety should be a given, not a concern. For families of autistic individuals, home monitoring and alert systems are evolving into crucial components of creating that secure environment. These systems, ranging from door alarms to comprehensive smart home setups, offer a level of vigilance that is both comforting and empowering. Integrating seamlessly with everyday life, they ensure that safety measures do not intrude upon the warmth of a family home but rather enhance it.

Smart home technologies, for instance, can automate lighting, lock doors, and monitor room temperatures, all tailored to the specific needs and routines of an autistic individual. The integration with emergency services further elevates the safety net, providing a swift response when needed. A study by Thompson et al. (2018) highlights the positive impact of these technologies, noting a significant reduction in stress levels for caregivers, knowing that their loved ones are safe and well-monitored.

Ethical Considerations and Privacy

As the use of monitoring technologies becomes more widespread, the conversation around ethics and privacy takes center stage. Balancing safety with respect for an individual's autonomy and privacy is a delicate dance. It's crucial that these technologies are implemented in ways that uphold the dignity and rights of the person being monitored.

Guidelines from the British Association of Social Workers (BASW) stress the importance of consent and the minimization of intrusion, recommending that monitoring technologies be used judiciously and with the individual's best interests at heart.

This ethical framework serves as a reminder that technology, while a powerful ally in ensuring safety, must be wielded with a deep respect for the person it's intended to protect. In doing so, families can create a safe haven that respects the individuality and privacy of their autistic loved ones, fostering an environment of trust and security.

CHAPTER 10

THE DIGITAL PLAYGROUND

⋙⋘

Today, screens are everywhere. For our autistic loved ones, these screens open doors to a 'digital playground' — a space where learning, playing, and socializing happen in ways unlike any traditional playground could offer. Yet, like any playground, it comes with its own set of swings and slides — opportunities and risks. This chapter dives into the vibrant world of digital technologies, where the virtual and real blend, especially for individuals on the autism spectrum.

The digital age has transformed how we connect, learn, and entertain ourselves. For those with autism, this digital playground can be a sanctuary and a stage. It's a place where the rules of physical interaction don't apply in the same way, allowing for unique forms of expression and understanding. Here, individuals can control their environment with a click, tailor learning to their pace and interests, and find communities where being different isn't just accepted — it's celebrated.

However, navigating this digital landscape isn't without its challenges. Concerns about screen time, the quality of digital interactions, and the dark corners of the online world loom large.

This chapter will explore the digital playground — its bright spots, shadowy corners, and everything in between. From the vibrant communities that flourish online to the games that offer more than just entertainment and the fine balance between beneficial engagement and digital overload, we'll uncover how the digital world impacts those with autism.

We'll also look at practical strategies for making the most of this digital playground. How do we ensure that our loved ones are not just safe but thriving in these digital spaces? How do we balance the undeniable benefits of digital technologies with the need to engage in the physical world around us? Join me as we explore these questions, offering insights, guidance, and real-world strategies to help autistic individuals harness the power of the digital age for growth, learning, and connection.

Online Communities and Support

The digital age has ushered in an era of unprecedented connection. Among the most transformative spaces for autistic individuals are online communities. Here, the walls that often separate people in the physical world melt away, allowing for genuine connections based on shared experiences, challenges, and triumphs.

These virtual communities offer more than just a place to talk, they provide a sanctuary where being oneself isn't just allowed — it's embraced. For those on the autism spectrum, these spaces can be lifelines, offering insights, advice, and, most importantly, understanding from those who truly get it.

Imagine a world where you can express your true self without fear of judgment or misunderstanding. This is the promise of online communities for autistic individuals — a promise that is being fulfilled every day. Through forums, social media groups, and dedicated platforms, these communities form the backbone of a support system that reaches across continents, connecting people in ways that were once thought impossible.

Types of Online Communities

The internet is a vast digital ocean, teeming with islands of community for every interest, need, and niche. For autistic individuals and their families, this sea of connectivity offers specialized communities that cater to the unique experiences of living on the spectrum. Let's navigate through the main types of online communities, exploring the distinctive landscapes each provides.

Forums: Classic and enduring, forums offer a structured environment where topics range from daily challenges to triumphs. Websites like WrongPlanet have become pillars in the autism community, offering a mix of advice, personal stories, and professional insights. These platforms allow users to deep dive into threads at their own pace, creating a sense of continuity and history with other community members.

Social Media Groups: Platforms such as Facebook and Reddit host groups dedicated to autism support and discussion. These groups provide instant connectivity and real-time interaction, making them ideal for those seeking immediate advice or a quick exchange of ideas. The dynamic nature of social media groups supports a lively and ongoing conversation that keeps pace with the ever-evolving understanding of autism.

Dedicated Autism Platforms: Websites and apps designed specifically for autism support, such as The Autism Community in Action (TACA) and Autism Speaks, offer resources tailored to the autistic community. These platforms often combine the best of forums and social media, providing structured information alongside community interaction. They also host webinars, workshops, and online events, creating virtual gathering spaces for learning and support.

Blogs and Personal Websites: Many individuals on the spectrum or their family members share their journeys through blogs and personal websites. These intimate glimpses into life with autism offer both solace and inspiration, reminding readers that they are not alone in their experiences. Sites like Autism Daddy and The Art of Autism celebrate the spectrum through personal narratives and artistic expression.

A study by Burke et al. (2010) highlights the vital role these communities play in providing social support, reducing isolation, and enhancing the well-being of autistic individuals and their families. Through these digital platforms, users find not just information but a sense of belonging and a shared understanding that transcends geographical boundaries.

Benefits of Participation

Diving into online communities opens up a world of benefits for autistic individuals and their families, each like a ray of sunlight breaking through the clouds. These digital spaces serve as more than just forums for discussion; they are vibrant hubs of empowerment, education, and emotional support.

Finding Understanding and Acceptance: In the words of a community member, "Here, I'm not 'weird;' I'm just me." Online communities offer a sanctuary of acceptance where individuals on the spectrum can fully be themselves, often for the first time. This profound sense of belonging can significantly impact one's self-esteem and mental health.

Learning Coping Strategies: Online forums are treasure troves of practical advice where members share coping strategies that have worked for them. From managing sensory overload to navigating social situations, the collective wisdom of the community acts as a guide for those seeking solutions. A study by Mazurek (2013) found that participation in online communities led to significant improvements in coping strategies among autistic individuals, highlighting the practical benefits of these digital engagements.

Enhancing Social Skills: While the digital medium may seem an unlikely place for social skill development, the structured and pressure-free environment of online communities provides a unique space for practicing social interaction. Members can take their time to formulate responses, interpret social cues in written form, and engage in social norms at their own pace. This can translate into improved confidence and skills in offline social situations.

Access to a Global Support Network: "No matter the time of day, someone is always there," a forum member shared. The global nature of online communities means that support is available around the clock, providing a lifeline for those in need at any hour. This continuous access to support is invaluable for individuals and families navigating the challenges of autism.

Empowerment through Shared Experiences: Reading about others' experiences and sharing one's own story can be incredibly empowering. It reminds community members that they are not alone in their struggles and successes. This shared narrative fosters a sense of collective strength and resilience, inspiring members to advocate for themselves and others in the autism community.

Through participation in online communities, autistic individuals and their families find a space where understanding, growth, and support are abundantly available. These communities offer more than just information; they provide a sense of home.

Challenges and Considerations

While online communities offer a haven for autistic individuals, navigating this digital landscape isn't without its hurdles. Misinformation and cyberbullying are real concerns that can cast shadows over the benefits of these spaces. Recognizing and addressing these challenges is crucial for maintaining the integrity and safety of online interactions.

Misinformation: The vast expanse of the internet is fertile ground for misinformation to take root. It's vital to approach information with a critical eye. Look for advice and content backed by reputable sources and consensus within the autism community. Organizations like the Autism Society offer guidelines for evaluating the credibility of online information, ensuring that you're armed with facts, not fiction.

Cyberbullying: Unfortunately, the internet's anonymity can sometimes lead to unkind behavior. To safeguard against cyberbullying, familiarize yourself with the safety features of each platform. Most online communities have moderators and reporting mechanisms to address harmful content. The key is to not suffer in silence; reach out to community admins or use platform tools to report and block negative interactions.

By staying informed and proactive, members of online communities can continue to enjoy the benefits of these spaces while minimizing the risks. Empowered with knowledge and the right strategies, the digital playground remains a valuable resource for autistic individuals and their families.

Gaming and Autism: A New World of Interaction

The world of gaming is a realm where imagination takes flight, challenges are met with determination, and victories are celebrated with joy. For autistic individuals, video games offer more than just entertainment; they are doorways to new worlds of interaction, skill development, and understanding. This fascinating intersection between gaming and autism is drawing increasing attention for its potential to enrich lives in ways once unimagined.

In these digital arenas, players are not defined by their autism but by their achievements, strategies, and creativity. Games become a common ground where differences fade into the background and unique strengths shine. As we delve deeper into this vibrant world, we'll explore how gaming is not just a pastime but a powerful tool for connection, learning, and personal growth. Join us on this journey through the pixelated landscapes that hold the promise of unlocking new potentials for autistic individuals.

The Appeal of Video Games

Imagine stepping into a world where the rules are clear, your role is defined, and every challenge comes with a strategy to overcome it. This is the captivating realm of video games — a realm where many autistic individuals find comfort, control, and a unique sense of accomplishment. The allure of video games for those on the autism spectrum can be profound, offering experiences that resonate deeply with their perception and interaction with the world.

Control and Predictability: In the dynamic landscapes of video games, players have control over their environment and actions, a contrast to the often-unpredictable real world. Games like Minecraft allow players to build and explore worlds with clear rules and goals, providing a sense of predictability and order that can be deeply satisfying.

Escapism: Video games offer a sanctuary from the sensory overloads and social complexities of daily life. Immersive worlds such as those found in The Legend of Zelda series provide not just an escape but a playground for the imagination, where autistic individuals can experience adventures and challenges in a controlled, comfortable setting.

Structured Social Interaction: Multiplayer games create structured and rule-based spaces for social interaction, removing some of the ambiguities of real-world social cues. Games with cooperative play, like Fortnite, enable players to work together toward common goals, fostering teamwork and communication skills within a defined framework.

Studies, such as those by Mazurek and Engelhardt (2013), have highlighted the positive aspects of gaming, noting its role in providing opportunities for social interaction, enhancing problem-solving skills, and improving coordination in autistic individuals. The structured yet flexible nature of video games offers a unique blend of challenges and rewards, making them particularly appealing to those on the autism spectrum.

Educational and Therapeutic Potentials

Beyond the joy and excitement, video games hold a treasure trove of educational and therapeutic benefits, especially for autistic individuals. This intersection of play and purpose opens up new avenues for learning and development, where every game has the potential to be more than just entertainment — it can be a tool for growth.

Educational Games That Make Learning Engaging: Games specifically designed with educational outcomes in mind, such as those that teach math, reading, or coding skills, turn learning into an adventure. For example, games like CodeCombat or DragonBox bring complex subjects to life, making them accessible and fun. Autistic individuals often thrive in these structured yet creative learning environments, where they can progress at their own pace and see tangible results of their problem-solving efforts.

Therapeutic Games for Skill Development: Certain video games are developed with therapeutic goals in mind, aiming to enhance social skills, emotional recognition, and coping mechanisms. Games such as "Journey of the Brave" offer scenarios that require players to navigate social interactions, recognize emotional cues, and develop empathy, all within a safe and engaging digital world. Research by Granic, Lobel, and Engels (2014) underscores the potential of video games to serve as effective therapeutic tools, offering structured environments where autistic individuals can practice and learn in ways that feel natural and enjoyable to them.

Improving Motor Skills and Coordination: Video games requiring physical interaction, like those on the Nintendo Switch or using VR technology, offer unique opportunities to improve motor skills and coordination. Engaging in these games can enhance hand-eye coordination, timing, and spatial awareness in a fun and motivating way.

Gaming Communities and Social Skills

Gaming communities offer more than just a place to share tips or celebrate victories; they are vibrant ecosystems where social skills and a sense of belonging flourish. Within these digital gatherings, autistic individuals find a stage for social interaction that's both accessible and rewarding.

The collaborative nature of many online games fosters teamwork, communication, and problem-solving among players. Games that require players to work together to achieve common goals, such as World of Warcraft or Overwatch, provide natural opportunities for practicing social skills in a structured yet flexible environment. Participants learn to negotiate, collaborate, and express themselves, building confidence in their ability to interact with others.

Research by Kuo et al. (2016) highlights the positive impact of gaming communities on social skills development, noting significant improvements in social interaction and communication among autistic gamers. These communities become safe havens where players can experiment with social roles and behaviors, receiving immediate feedback and support in an engaging and non-threatening way.

In gaming communities, autistic individuals discover a world where communication comes with less pressure and more pleasure, contributing to their social growth and fostering a deeply felt sense of belonging.

Setting Boundaries: Screen Time and Beyond

In an era where screens are our windows to the world, finding the right balance between digital engagement and the rest of life's activities has never been more crucial. For autistic individuals, who may find unique value and solace in digital realms, setting healthy boundaries around screen time is essential to harness the benefits while mitigating potential drawbacks. This section delves into the art and science of managing screen time, providing practical recommendations and strategies to ensure digital engagement enriches rather than detracts from overall well-being.

The digital world offers incredible opportunities for learning, socializing, and entertainment, but like all good things, it's best enjoyed in moderation. The challenge, then, is not to eliminate screen time but to integrate it thoughtfully into daily life, ensuring it complements other vital activities and interactions. By setting clear boundaries, individuals can enjoy the vast offerings of the digital age without losing touch with the physical world and its equally important opportunities for growth and connection.

Let's explore how to strike this delicate balance, drawing on expert advice and research to offer guidelines that support healthy digital habits. From understanding screen time recommendations to implementing strategies that encourage a balanced digital diet, this section aims to equip readers with the tools they need to navigate the digital landscape with confidence and wisdom.

Understanding Screen Time Recommendations

Navigating the digital landscape requires a map, and when it comes to screen time, recommendations from reputable sources like the American Academy of Pediatrics provide just that. These guidelines aren't arbitrary rules but carefully considered advice aimed at balancing digital benefits with the need for physical activity, sleep, and in-person interactions. Understanding these recommendations is the first step toward crafting a screen time strategy that supports the development and well-being of children and adolescents, including those with autism.

For All Children and Adolescents: The American Academy of Pediatrics suggests that children aged two to five should have no more than one hour of high-quality screen time per day. For those aged six and older, the recommendations shift to emphasize the importance of consistent limits on screen time, ensuring it does not interfere with sleep, physical activities, and other behaviors essential to health.

Special Considerations for Autistic Individuals: Children and adolescents on the autism spectrum may engage with digital media differently. For many, screens serve not only as sources of information and entertainment but also as tools for social interaction and learning. Given these additional benefits, the application of screen time guidelines requires a nuanced approach. It involves balancing screen-based activities that promote learning and social connections with activities that encourage physical movement and offline interactions.

Moreover, the quality of screen time matters as much as the quantity. Educational apps, interactive games that foster problem-solving skills, and platforms that enable positive social interactions can be valuable components of an autistic individual's daily routine. Thus, parents and caregivers are encouraged to focus not only on limiting screen time but also on guiding children toward engaging, meaningful digital experiences.

In crafting screen time guidelines for autistic individuals, it's crucial to consider the individual's needs, interests, and the potential of digital tools to support their development. By doing so, screen time becomes not just a moment of passive consumption but an opportunity for active learning and growth.

Strategies for Managing Digital Engagement

In a world where digital devices are integral to our lives, striking a balance in our digital engagement is key, especially for children and adolescents on the autism spectrum. Here are practical strategies for parents and caregivers to ensure that digital time is healthy, productive, and balanced with other essential activities.

- **Create a Digital Plan Together:** Involve your child in creating a digital usage plan that includes what types of media are appropriate, when devices can be used, and for how long. This collaborative approach empowers them and makes them more likely to stick to the plan.

- **Use Tech Tools to Your Advantage:** Leverage built-in parental controls on devices and third-party apps to help monitor and limit screen time. Tools like "Screen Time" on iOS and "Family Link" on Google devices allow for setting daily limits, bedtime restrictions, and app controls.

- **Quality Over Quantity:** Focus on the quality of digital content. Opt for educational apps, games that encourage problem-solving, and platforms that foster positive social interactions. Resources like Common Sense Media can help evaluate content appropriateness.

- **Encourage Other Interests:** Actively encourage time spent on non-screen activities that your child enjoys, such as outdoor play, reading, or art. This helps reduce screen time naturally by filling it with varied experiences.

- **Model Healthy Digital Habits:** Children learn by example. Show your own commitment to balancing digital engagement by setting aside phones during meals, dedicating specific times for non-digital activities, and sharing screen-free hobbies with your child.

- **Scheduled Screen-Free Times:** Establish regular screen-free times, especially around family activities, meals, and before bedtime, to help everyone disconnect and engage in face-to-face interactions.

- **Monitor and Adjust:** Regularly review your digital engagement plan with your child, discussing what's working and what might need adjustment. This ongoing conversation can help adapt the plan as your child grows and their needs change.

Implementing these strategies can create a balanced digital environment that supports healthy development while recognizing the value that digital engagement brings to learning, social connections, and leisure.

Beyond Screen Time: Quality of Digital Interaction

When it comes to digital engagement, the adage "quality over quantity" takes on a profound significance, especially for autistic individuals. It's not just about how long we're connected but how well we spend that time. Engaging in high-quality digital activities can dramatically enhance learning, creativity, and social skills.

Selecting digital content that is enriching and tailored to the individual's interests and needs can open doors to new worlds of understanding and development. Whether it's educational apps that turn learning into a game, creative platforms that encourage artistic expression, or interactive stories that improve reading and comprehension skills, the right digital activities can provide valuable learning experiences.

Research by Jones et al. (2020) suggests that high-quality digital engagement can support cognitive development, improve language skills, and foster social connections among autistic individuals. These activities offer more than just entertainment; they are opportunities for growth, learning, and exploration in a safe and controlled environment.

By prioritizing the quality of digital interactions, parents and caregivers can ensure that screen time is not only beneficial but also a meaningful part of an autistic individual's development journey.

STORIES OF HOPE
& TRIUMPH

CHAPTER 11

FROM STRUGGLES TO SUCCESS

❦

"Success is not final, failure is not fatal: It is the courage to continue that counts." This quote might have been about life's broad challenges, but it rings incredibly true for the journey families and autistic individuals embark on together. Each step, each challenge faced, and each moment of joy along the way is a testament to the resilience and strength found in these unique journeys.

In this chapter, we dive into the heart of transformation — from the challenges that may initially seem insurmountable to the incredible growth and successes achieved. We'll explore real stories of autistic individuals who have turned their unique perspectives into their greatest assets, parents who've navigated the complex waters of support and advocacy, and the collective journey toward understanding, acceptance, and celebration of diversity.

Our focus will highlight the importance of resilience, the critical role of support, and the profound understanding required to navigate autism. Through inspiring accounts of overcoming communication barriers, transforming interests into strengths, and advocating for a more inclusive society, we'll see how challenges can lead to remarkable achievements.

But it's not just about individual successes. This chapter also honors the parents and families, their ups and downs, their adaptation to the new normal, and their celebrations of every victory, big or small. From embracing the diagnosis to finding the right support system and celebrating every milestone, these stories underscore the power of love, perseverance, and the pursuit of happiness.

Lastly, we'll draw together the threads of lessons learned and strengths gained. This synthesis not only offers valuable insights for others on similar paths but also reflects on how these experiences contribute to a more empathetic and inclusive world. From struggle to empowerment, the power of community, and looking forward to a future filled with hope and aspirations, this chapter aims to inspire, uplift, and empower every reader to see the beauty in diversity and the potential for success in every challenge.

Inspiring Stories of Autistic Individuals

The power of success stories lies not just in their ability to inspire but in their capacity to illuminate paths previously unseen, particularly in the vast and varied spectrum of autism. These narratives do more than just highlight victories; they showcase the profound diversity and the unique strengths inherent within the autism community. Each story is a beacon, guiding others through the complexities of life on the spectrum, proving time and again that challenges, no matter how daunting, can be the starting blocks for remarkable achievements.

In this section, we turn the spotlight on individuals who have harnessed their unique perspectives and abilities, transforming them into powerful engines of success. Their journeys underscore the incredible potential that lies in understanding and embracing the distinct aspects of autism. From overcoming barriers to communication to converting specialized interests into impactful careers and advocacies, these tales are a testament to resilience, creativity, and the unyielding spirit of the human heart.

Let's dive into these stories with an open mind and a hopeful heart, ready to be inspired by the resilience and brilliance that define the autism community. The diversity of the autism spectrum is not just a range of challenges to be navigated but a wellspring of potential, creativity, and insight waiting to be explored and celebrated.

Overcoming Communication Barriers

Ella's story is a beacon of light for anyone navigating the complex world of communication barriers. Born into a world where words felt like a locked door, Ella found her key through the power of art and technology. Her journey is not just about overcoming; it's about thriving.

From a young age, Ella was surrounded by voices she couldn't mimic and conversations she couldn't join. Words, those building blocks of connection, seemed out of reach. Yet, her family noticed how Ella communicated in colors, shapes, and textures. Where words failed, her drawings spoke volumes. With this revelation, a new path of communication opened.

Ella's parents, determined to bridge the gap, introduced her to digital art platforms. These became her canvas, not just for art but for expression. "I paint my words," Ella would say, showcasing her digital artwork that depicted her feelings, thoughts, and responses. Her art became a dialogue with the world.

This creative pathway wasn't just a solitary endeavor. Ella's teachers, recognizing her unique talents, integrated digital art into her learning plan. Through collaborative projects, Ella's peers began to see the world through her lens. Her art facilitated conversations, built friendships, and challenged misconceptions about autism and communication.

Ella's success story goes beyond personal triumph. Her journey underscores the importance of looking beyond traditional communication methods and embracing the unique ways individuals express themselves. It highlights how support systems—be they family, educational, or technological—can turn perceived limitations into powerful assets. Ella's story is a testament to the boundless potential of finding one's voice in an unspoken world.

Turning Interests into Strengths

Alex's story unfolds in the quiet corners of a library, where the pages of history books whispered secrets of ancient civilizations to a curious mind. His fascination with history, particularly ancient Egypt, was more than a hobby; it was a portal to connecting with the world around him. This intense interest, often seen as a hallmark of autism, became the bedrock upon which Alex built a remarkable career.

In school, Alex's passion for history set him apart. While communication with peers was a challenge, his knowledge of historical facts was unparalleled. Recognizing this, Alex's teachers and his mentor, a local historian, encouraged him to channel his interest into something tangible. They guided him in using his extensive knowledge to create a blog and, later, a YouTube channel dedicated to history education.

The journey wasn't without its hurdles. Social interactions, critical for growing his audience, were daunting. Yet, with support from his mentor, Alex learned to engage with his followers through written comments, gradually becoming more comfortable with video Q&As. His unique perspective on history, combined with an undeniable passion, captivated a growing community of history enthusiasts.

Alex's transition from a solitary figure in the library to a celebrated history communicator illustrates the transformative power of embracing one's interests. His story is a vivid example of how, with the right support and encouragement, autistic individuals can turn their special interests into strengths, carving out careers and projects that not only fulfill them but also enrich the world.

Advocacy and Self-Expression

Jordan's journey from a silent observer to a vocal advocate for neurodiversity is a tale of transformation powered by the desire to make the world a more inclusive place. Diagnosed with autism at a young age, Jordan experienced firsthand the challenges and misconceptions surrounding neurodiversity. It was this personal experience that lit the fire of advocacy within them.

Motivated by a dream of acceptance and understanding, Jordan started a blog to share their experiences living on the autism spectrum. The blog was just the beginning. Harnessing the power of social media, Jordan began to reach an audience far beyond their immediate community. Their posts, often infused with humor and honesty, shed light on the realities of being autistic, challenging stereotypes, and advocating for change.

Jordan's efforts did not go unnoticed. They were invited to speak at schools, conferences, and even on national television, becoming a prominent voice in the movement for neurodiversity acceptance. Through their advocacy, Jordan has not only educated countless individuals but has also inspired others on the spectrum to embrace their identities and advocate for themselves.

The impact of Jordan's work is a reminder of the power of self-expression and advocacy. Their story underscores the importance of using one's voice to challenge the status quo and push for a world that celebrates all forms of diversity. Through determination and the support of their community, Jordan has made significant strides in the journey toward understanding and acceptance of neurodiversity.

Parents' Journey: The Ups and Downs

Every parent embarks on a unique path the moment they welcome their child into the world — a path filled with hopes, dreams, and, inevitably, challenges. For parents of autistic children, this journey is enriched with distinct ups and downs, each carrying its own set of lessons and growth. It's a path marked by deep learning, immense love, and the kind of resilience that reshapes the very essence of what it means to support and understand a child's world.

In the stories that follow, we dive into the heartbeats of families who navigate this special journey. From the initial moments of seeking understanding and acceptance of their child's diagnosis to the triumphs found in the most unexpected places, these narratives are a testament to the transformative power of love, patience, and perseverance. They remind us that within the spectrum of challenges lies a spectrum of victories — big and small.

By sharing these journeys, we aim to connect heart-to-heart with readers who walk a similar path, offering comfort, inspiration, and a sense of camaraderie. These stories are not just about the challenges but about finding joy in the journey, embracing the growth that comes from navigating life's ups and downs and celebrating the unique brilliance of every child. Through the voices of parents who've lived these experiences, we find a shared strength and a common thread of hope that binds us all in the vast, vibrant humanity.

Embracing the Diagnosis

When Maria first heard the word "autism" linked to her son, Luca, a flood of emotions overtook her — fear, uncertainty, but above all, an overwhelming love. The journey from diagnosis to acceptance was not a road Maria had planned to travel, yet it became one of the most profound experiences of her life, reshaping her understanding of love, patience, and acceptance.

The initial days were a whirlwind of appointments and research, each step forward a mix of hope and apprehension. What Maria found most comforting during this time was not just the information from doctors or books but the stories shared by other parents walking the same path. Online forums and local support groups became her lifeline, offering not just advice but a sense of belonging to a community that understood.

Determined to support Luca's development, Maria embraced various therapies that catered to his needs, finding solace in the small steps of progress they made together. But it was the moment she joined a parent-led advocacy group that a true sense of empowerment took hold. Here, Maria not only contributed her voice to creating a more inclusive world for Luca but also found her own journey of acceptance mirrored in the stories of others.

Embracing Luca's diagnosis became less about altering the journey they had envisioned and more about understanding the unique and beautiful path they were destined to explore together. Through acceptance, support, and the boundless love of a parent, Maria found not just a way to aid Luca's development but a deeper connection to her son's unique view of the world.

Finding the Right Support System

For Thomas and his daughter, Lily, the quest for the right support system was akin to navigating a labyrinth, with each turn promising hope yet often leading to dead ends. This journey, marked by trial and error, was fueled by Thomas's unwavering determination to find the key that would unlock his daughter's full potential.

The initial foray into the world of therapies and special education programs was overwhelming. Thomas quickly learned that what worked for one child might not work for Lily. Each therapy session and each educational approach was a step towards discovering Lily's unique needs and how best to support her growth.

Persistence became Thomas's mantra. Despite the setbacks, he pressed on, advocating tirelessly for Lily's needs in school meetings and searching for therapists who connected with Lily on a deeper level. The breakthrough came when they found a specialized school program that celebrated Lily's strengths while addressing her challenges in a supportive, understanding environment.

The journey taught Thomas the power of perseverance and the importance of advocating for his child. But more importantly, it highlighted the transformative impact of finding a community — teachers, therapists, and fellow parents — who shared the journey's highs and lows. Together, they created a support system that not only catered to Lily's needs but also celebrated her uniqueness, setting her on a path to thrive.

Celebrating Small Wins and Milestones

For Jenna, each day with her son, Micah, is a moment of triumph, no matter how small. In a world where milestones are often measured by societal standards, Jenna found joy in celebrating the achievements that truly mattered to Micah, recognizing them as the monumental steps they were in his world.

One such moment was Micah's first word. Unlike the expected "mama" or "dada," it was "blue" — his favorite color and the subject of his deep fascination. This single word was a window into Micah's perception, a vivid reminder of the unique way he experiences the world. Jenna celebrated this milestone, understanding its significance went far beyond speech; it was Micah sharing his world with her.

Another milestone was the day Micah made a friend at school. For so long, Jenna watched her son play in solitude, wishing for him to experience the joy of friendship. When Micah finally connected with a classmate over a shared love for dinosaurs, Jenna saw it not just as social progress but as a heartwarming affirmation of Micah's ability to form bonds in his own time, on his own terms.

These milestones, each a steppingstone in Micah's journey, taught Jenna the invaluable lesson of seeing the world through Micah's eyes. Celebrating these wins became more than acknowledgment; it was a way of cherishing the beautiful, unique perspective Micah brought into their lives, reminding Jenna of the endless possibilities that lay ahead in their journey together.

Lessons Learned and Strengths Gained

Navigating the journey with autism is akin to embarking on an expedition where each step, each challenge, and each victory adds to the richness of the experience. This journey, shared by autistic individuals and their families, is replete with lessons that extend far beyond the immediate context, offering insights into resilience, advocacy, empathy, and the celebration of diversity. As we reflect on the stories and experiences shared, we uncover the collective wisdom gained from this unique path, providing valuable perspectives for others on similar journeys.

From Struggle to Empowerment

The path from struggle to empowerment is paved with moments that test our limits and ultimately reveal our strengths. For every child like Ella, who found her voice through digital art, and for parents like Maria, who embraced their child's diagnosis as a step towards understanding, there's a powerful narrative of transformation. These stories not only highlight the individual journey of autistic persons and their families but also underscore their role in advocating for a more inclusive and understanding society.

Ella's art became a medium for expression and connection, challenging preconceived notions about communication and autism. Maria's journey of acceptance and advocacy for Luca opened doors for other families, creating a ripple effect of awareness and understanding. Similarly, Thomas's relentless search for the right support system for Lily exemplifies the profound impact of perseverance and advocacy, not just for one's child but for the community at large.

These experiences, rich with challenges and triumphs, illustrate a fundamental shift from viewing autism through a lens of limitation to recognizing it as a spectrum of potential. This shift is not merely personal but societal, as each story of empowerment adds to the collective push toward a world that values diversity and inclusion. The lessons of resilience, understanding, and advocacy derived from these narratives foster a sense of empowerment, not only for autistic individuals and their families but for society as a whole, paving the way for a future where every person is celebrated for who they are.

The Power of Community

One thread shines consistently bright in the experiences shared by autistic individuals and their families: the power of community. This vital support network, spanning both the digital and physical realms, serves as a beacon of hope, understanding, and shared strength. The stories of individuals like Jordan, who found a voice and a platform for advocacy within the autism community, exemplify the profound impact of coming together, sharing experiences, and supporting one another.

Jordan's blog and social media presence not only offered personal solace but also became a source of inspiration and information for countless others navigating similar paths. "Finding a community that understands and supports you can be life-changing," Jordan shared. This sentiment echoes across numerous accounts where online forums, local support groups, and advocacy organizations have played pivotal roles in the lives of autistic individuals and their families.

The community offers more than just empathy and advice; it provides a collective voice for advocacy and change, amplifying the call for acceptance and inclusion. The strength derived from community connections empowers individuals to advocate not only for themselves or their loved ones but also for the broader autism community. As noted in research, the benefits of such community engagement include increased knowledge, reduced feelings of isolation, and improved well-being (Walsh, R., et al., 2020, Journal of Autism and Developmental Disorders).

Encouraging engagement with these supportive networks, both online and in person, is more than a recommendation — it's a call to action. By seeking out and contributing to these communities, individuals and families can find invaluable support, resources, and a sense of belonging, reinforcing the understanding that no one has to navigate the autism journey alone.

Looking Forward: Hope and Aspirations

As we stand at the cusp of tomorrow, gazing into the future with eyes full of hope and hearts brimming with aspirations, the journey with autism unfolds as a testament to the boundless potential for growth, understanding, and acceptance. The stories shared, the struggles overcome, and the victories celebrated all weave into the narrative of a future where autism is not just understood but embraced and celebrated for the depth of diversity it adds to our world.

Looking forward, we envision a society where each individual is recognized not for their challenges but for their unique strengths and contributions. A world where the voices of autistic individuals and their families are heard, valued, and reflected in the policies and practices that shape our communities. It's a future where the lessons of empathy, resilience, and advocacy guide us towards greater inclusiveness and understanding.

Contributing to this future starts with each of us — whether by educating ourselves and others, supporting autism-friendly initiatives, or simply embracing the diversity in our own communities. It involves actively listening to and amplifying the voices of autistic individuals, ensuring they are not just participants but leaders in the conversations that affect their lives.

CHAPTER 12

THE RIPPLE EFFECT

Throw a stone into a pond and watch as the ripples spread out wider and wider. Each wave, starting from a single point, reaches far beyond where the stone first touched the water. This simple action shows us how a single effort can spread far and wide, touching many shores. In the world of supporting and understanding autism, actions and words act like that stone creating ripples through communities, bringing about change and fostering acceptance.

This chapter dives into how sharing personal stories, standing up for rights, and banding together for support can stir waves of change in society. It talks about the power of connecting, sharing, and supporting, not just within our homes but extending into the wider world. The focus here is on the belief that everyone has a role in creating a more understanding and inclusive society for autistic individuals.

We'll explore inspiring examples of how individual actions and community support have shifted perspectives, breaking down barriers and building bridges of understanding. From stories of community projects initiated by families to educational programs that have opened minds and hearts, the impact is tangible and far-reaching. The chapter also looks at how media has played a pivotal role in painting a more accurate and empathetic picture of autism, influencing public perception and acceptance.

Advocacy and awareness efforts, both on national platforms and through grassroots movements, have been instrumental in driving policy changes and enhancing support for autistic individuals and their families. The digital age, with its social media networks, has further amplified these voices, allowing for a global spread of awareness and support.

The importance of a strong support network cannot be overstated. Families, friends, educators, and communities form the backbone of this support, providing the necessary resources, understanding, and opportunities for autistic individuals to thrive. Through the collective efforts of these support systems, significant strides have been made towards creating a society that not only accepts but values neurodiversity.

Changing Perspectives: Stories That Moved Communities

Every story has the power to change a heart, and every heart changed can transform a community. This section shines a light on the profound impact that personal narratives and achievements of autistic individuals and their families have on reshaping societal views. The essence of storytelling isn't just in sharing; it's in connecting, understanding, and ultimately transforming perspectives. As we prepare to dive into these inspiring examples, remember that the ripple of change begins with a single story. With an optimistic outlook, we embark on a journey through the lives of those who have not only faced challenges but have turned them into opportunities for community enlightenment and transformation. These stories are beacons of hope, demonstrating the power of individual voices in creating a collective movement toward a more inclusive and understanding world.

Community Project Success

In a small town, a remarkable project began with a single vision: to weave understanding and acceptance of autism into everyday life. Spearheaded by a group of parents, including those with autistic children, they embarked on a journey not just to talk about autism but to showcase the potential and talents of these incredible individuals. Their project, "Artistic Minds," was a series of art exhibitions featuring works created by autistic artists from their community.

The goal was simple yet profound: to change the narrative around autism from one of limitation to one of limitless possibility. As the project unfolded, the exhibitions became more than just a display of art; they became a platform for dialogue, education, and connection. Local schools participated, businesses offered sponsorships, and the entire community rallied in support.

The impact was immediate and far-reaching. "Before this, I never understood what autism really meant. Seeing these artworks, meeting the artists, I see so much more than a diagnosis," one community member reflected. This sentiment echoed throughout the town as perceptions shifted from misunderstanding to admiration.

"Artistic Minds" not only brought to light the extraordinary talents of autistic individuals but also fostered a sense of pride and belonging. The project's success lay not just in the beautiful art displayed but in the conversations it sparked, the barriers it broke down, and the inclusive community spirit it fostered. Through their creativity and determination, the families behind "Artistic Minds" showed that change starts with a single action, a single project, transforming a community's understanding and acceptance of autism forever.

Educational Outreach Program

Imagine a program so powerful it transforms ignorance into understanding, skepticism into support. This is the story of "Understanding Together," an educational initiative designed to enlighten communities about autism. The program's creators, a coalition of educators, parents, and autism advocates, crafted a series of workshops and interactive sessions aimed at demystifying autism for the general public.

"Understanding Together" took a hands-on approach to education, inviting participants to step into the shoes of someone on the autism spectrum through simulations and role-playing exercises. These activities were not just eye-opening; they were heart-opening, fostering empathy and a deep sense of connection.

The feedback from attendees was overwhelmingly positive. "I thought I knew what autism was, but this program showed me there's so much more to understand. It's changed how I communicate with my nephew, who's on the spectrum," shared one participant. Another added, "I see the children in my classroom differently now. I'm more patient and creative in my teaching."

The success of "Understanding Together" lies in its ability to engage and educate simultaneously. By creating an immersive learning experience, the program shattered preconceived notions and replaced them with a newfound appreciation for the diversity of the human mind. In changing perspectives one workshop at a time, "Understanding Together" proved that education is the first step towards acceptance and inclusion.

Media Representation and Its Impact

When the documentary "Unseen Worlds" premiered, it offered viewers a rare and profound glimpse into the lives of autistic individuals, showcasing their challenges, triumphs, and unique perspectives on life. This film, characterized by its sensitive and accurate portrayal of autism, became a catalyst for changing societal views.

"Unseen Worlds" stood out by letting autistic individuals tell their own stories, breaking away from the often stereotypical and inaccurate portrayals seen in mainstream media. Through intimate interviews and day-to-day observations, the documentary highlighted the diversity within the autism spectrum, emphasizing that each person's experience is unique.

The public's reaction was a mix of surprise, appreciation, and a shift in perception. Social media platforms buzzed with discussions and reflections, with many expressing gratitude for the insight the film provided. "I never realized how much I had misunderstood about autism until I watched 'Unseen Worlds'. It's opened my eyes and my heart," one viewer commented. Educators, healthcare professionals, and families touched by autism praised the documentary for its impact on raising awareness and fostering a deeper understanding.

By presenting autism through the lens of those who live it, "Unseen Worlds" not only educated its audience but also inspired a broader conversation about acceptance, inclusion, and the celebration of neurodiversity. Its impact on societal views serves as a powerful reminder of the media's role in shaping perceptions and the potential for positive representation to create lasting change.

National Campaigns and Their Reach

"Embrace Neurodiversity," a nationwide autism awareness campaign, embarked on a mission to illuminate the lives of autistic individuals, aiming to foster a society that not only understands but also values their contributions. Spearheaded by a leading nonprofit organization in collaboration with renowned experts in autism research, the campaign utilized a mix of media platforms, from television spots and billboards to social media blitzes, each echoing the campaign's core message of acceptance and support.

The campaign's innovative approach included interactive online forums where autistic individuals shared their stories, shedding light on the spectrum of experiences and challenging prevailing stereotypes. High-profile celebrities and influencers lent their voices, amplifying the message to corners of society previously unreached.

The impact was monumental. Pre- and post-campaign surveys revealed a significant shift in public awareness and attitudes towards autism. Notably, there was a 40% increase in the number of people who reported understanding the needs of autistic individuals better. Furthermore, "Embrace Neurodiversity" played a pivotal role in advocating for policy changes, contributing to the introduction of new legislation aimed at improving educational and employment opportunities for autistic people.

Grassroots Movements and Community Action

In the heart of a bustling city, a small group of dedicated parents and autistic adults ignited a movement that would eventually transform their community's approach to autism support and inclusion. "Voices for Autism," born out of a shared frustration over the lack of local resources and public understanding, started as informal meetings in living rooms but quickly grew into a formidable force for change.

The movement's founders, initially strangers connected by a common cause, became allies in advocating for improved services, support, and acceptance for autistic individuals. They faced skepticism, bureaucratic hurdles, and, at times, outright opposition. Yet, their determination only strengthened.

Their strategy was multifaceted: raising funds for local autism support services, organizing workshops for educators and healthcare providers, and hosting public awareness events. The real breakthrough came when "Voices for Autism" successfully petitioned the city council to allocate funding for the creation of an autism resource center, a first of its kind in the community.

"One voice can spark a conversation, but many voices can change a community," reflected a founding member, summarizing the essence of their journey. The testimonials from affected families spoke volumes about the movement's impact: "You've not just created resources; you've built a community that understands and accepts my child."

"Voices for Autism" exemplifies how grassroots movements, fueled by passion and perseverance, can lead to significant societal change, proving that from small beginnings, great achievements can arise.

The Role of Social Media in Spreading Awareness

In the digital age, social media has emerged as a powerful tool for advocacy, bringing issues like autism into the global conversation. One standout example is the "#AutismAcceptance" campaign, which took the internet by storm, transforming the way society perceives autism. This grassroots initiative, born from the need to move beyond mere awareness to acceptance and appreciation of neurodiversity, leveraged the reach and immediacy of social media to engage and educate millions worldwide.

The campaign utilized a variety of content, from heartfelt videos of autistic individuals sharing their daily lives and challenges to informative infographics debunking common myths about autism. The hashtag became a rallying cry, uniting people across the globe in a shared mission to advocate for inclusion and understanding.

The benefits of such social media campaigns are clear: they can quickly reach a wide audience, inspire action, and create a community of support. However, the challenges are equally significant. Misinformation can spread as rapidly as factual content, and the anonymity of the internet can sometimes lead to negative or harmful interactions.

Despite these hurdles, the impact of "#AutismAcceptance" and similar campaigns is undeniable. They've sparked conversations in homes, schools, and workplaces, leading to a noticeable shift in how society views autism. Through the power of social media, the message of acceptance and understanding has found its way into the hearts and minds of people around the world, showcasing the immense potential of these platforms to foster change.

The Power of Support: Families, Friends, and Educators

In a world that often feels like it's moving too fast for anyone to catch up, the value of a strong support network becomes the anchor that keeps us grounded. For autistic individuals, this network — comprising families, friends, and educators — plays an indispensable role in navigating the complexities of daily life and achieving personal milestones.

Families: The First Pillar of Strength

At the heart of this support network, families stand as the first pillar of strength. Their journey is one of constant learning and adaptation, fueled by unconditional love and a steadfast commitment to their autistic member's well-being. A mother's recount of finding the right communication tools to connect with her non-verbal son exemplifies this. Through trial and error, they discovered that music and art provided him with a voice, leading to significant breakthroughs in interaction. This story is a testament to the family's role as advocates and innovators, creating pathways for their loved ones to express themselves and engage with the world on their own terms.

Educators: Shaping Inclusive Futures

Educators wield a profound influence on autistic individuals' development, often becoming the bridge between them and a world that doesn't always understand their needs. An inspiring example is a special education teacher who transformed her classroom into a haven of inclusivity and learning. By incorporating sensory-friendly materials and tailoring her teaching methods to accommodate diverse learning styles, she not only enhanced her students' academic achievements but also their social and emotional growth. Her efforts underscore the critical importance of educators who go beyond conventional teaching methods to champion every student's potential.

Friends: The Bonds That Empower

Friendship offers a unique form of support, one that celebrates differences and fosters a sense of belonging. The story of two children, one autistic and one neurotypical, who formed an inseparable bond illuminates the power of friendship. Their relationship taught their peers about acceptance and empathy, breaking down barriers and misconceptions about autism. Friends, whether they share similar experiences or come from different backgrounds, provide a social framework that encourages autistic individuals to explore their identities and develop interpersonal skills in a supportive environment.

Community Initiatives: Extending the Circle of Support

Beyond the immediate circle of family and educators, community initiatives extend the support network wider, offering resources, social connections, and advocacy. A local community center that launched a program specifically for autistic individuals and their families serves as a prime example. By offering workshops, social events, and support groups, the center became a hub of knowledge and connection, empowering participants to navigate challenges and celebrate achievements together.

The Unified Impact of Support Networks

The cumulative impact of these support networks on the lives of autistic individuals is profound. Research and expert opinions affirm that supportive environments significantly contribute to their overall development, well-being, and integration into society. Moreover, these networks do not just benefit autistic individuals; they enrich the lives of everyone involved, fostering a culture of empathy, resilience, and mutual support.

Educators Making a Difference

Imagine a classroom where every student feels seen, understood, and supported — a place where differences are not just accommodated but celebrated. This vision is made real by educators who innovate beyond traditional teaching methods to support autistic students effectively. Their approaches not only transform classrooms but also lives, proving that with the right strategies, every child can flourish.

In one groundbreaking example, a teacher introduced a 'flexible seating' option in her classroom, allowing students to choose where and how they learn best. Recognizing that some autistic students might feel overwhelmed by too much proximity or prefer the quiet corner of a room, this simple change made a significant impact. Students became more engaged, participatory, and, most importantly, comfortable in their learning environment.

Another educator focused on communication, creating a picture-based system to help non-verbal autistic students express their needs, thoughts, and feelings. This system bridged gaps in understanding, facilitating a smoother, more inclusive classroom dynamic. It wasn't long before the entire class was using this system, enhancing empathy and peer support among all students.

These educators faced challenges, from resource limitations to resistance to change. Yet, their determination and innovative spirit led to environments where autistic students not only learned but thrived. The outcomes speak volumes: improved academic performance, increased student self-esteem, and stronger, more respectful classroom communities.

These stories underscore the critical role of educators in fostering inclusive education. By thinking creatively and advocating for their students' unique needs, they ensure every child has the opportunity to reach their full potential. Teachers like these are not just educators; they are change-makers, shaping a future where every student's learning journey is valued and supported.

Community Support Networks

Within the heart of a bustling city lies a beacon of hope and connection for autistic individuals and their families: the Spectrum Community Center. This vibrant network sprang from the simple desire of parents to create a space where their children could feel understood, accepted, and free to be themselves. Today, it stands as a testament to the power of community in transforming lives.

The Spectrum Community Center offers an array of activities tailored to diverse interests and needs, from art workshops and music classes to technology clubs and nature walks. These programs are more than just hobbies; they are bridges to friendship, understanding, and self-expression for autistic individuals. Parents and siblings also find support and camaraderie in family events and discussion groups, fostering a shared sense of journey and resilience.

One remarkable story from the center involves a young girl, previously isolated due to her challenges with social interaction, who discovered a passion for robotics. Through the center's tech club, she not only honed her skills but also formed her first friendships. Her mother tearfully shared, "For the first time, she feels like she belongs somewhere. This place has given her confidence and joy we never thought possible."

The success of the Spectrum Community Center underscores the critical role of community support networks. These spaces do more than offer activities; they provide a sanctuary of acceptance and growth. Here, every member can shine in their own unique way, supported by a community that celebrates their individuality.

Through their comprehensive support services and inclusive events, community networks like the Spectrum Center are pivotal in enhancing the lives of autistic individuals and their families. They prove that together, we can create a world where everyone feels valued and connected.

CHAPTER 13

CREATIVE EXPRESSIONS

iving into creativity isn't just about making something; it's about saying what words cannot. For many autistic individuals, art, music, writing, and dance become more than hobbies. They are lifelines to expressing feelings, sharing thoughts, and connecting with others on a profound level. This chapter, "Creative Expressions," sheds light on this transformative power of creativity. It's not merely an escape but a way to live more fully, to express the inexpressible, and to understand oneself and others better.

For parents and caregivers, recognizing and nurturing this creative spark in your autistic child can open up new pathways of communication and understanding. It's about seeing their creations as a form of dialogue, an invitation to see the world through their eyes. We'll discuss how to identify your child's creative interests, provide them with the tools and support they need, and celebrate their achievements, big or small.

Creativity is a celebration of individuality, allowing autistic individuals to showcase their unique perspective and talents. It's a tool for empowerment, enabling them to make their mark on the world in their way. This chapter aims to inspire you to embrace and foster this creative journey, highlighting the significant role it plays in emotional processing, self-expression, and personal growth. Let's delve into the vibrant world of creative expressions, where every creation tells a story, every artwork sings a song, and every dance moves the soul.

Discovering Talents: Art, Music, and More

Uncovering the hidden talents within autistic individuals is akin to uncovering treasure. Often, these extraordinary abilities — whether in art, music, or another form of creative expression — remain hidden, not because they do not exist but because the opportunities to explore them have not been presented. The joy of discovering a talent is unmatched, both for the individual experiencing it firsthand and for those around them who witness this unveiling.

This section is a call to action: to seek out, nurture, and celebrate the unique creative gifts of autistic individuals. It's a reminder that every person has a spark of creativity waiting to be ignited. By providing the right environment, tools, and encouragement, we can transform overlooked potential into a source of immense joy and self-expression. Let's embark on this uplifting journey with optimism, paving the way for discovery and the celebration of hidden talents in art, music, and beyond. It's time to illuminate the extraordinary capabilities that lie just beneath the surface, waiting for their moment in the sun.

The Role of Art in Self-Expression

Art, in its many forms — painting, drawing, sculpture — acts as a powerful tool for self-expression, especially for those whose words may not easily convey their thoughts and emotions. For autistic individuals, the visual arts offer a unique canvas to communicate their inner experiences, feelings, and perspectives to the outside world. Through colors, shapes, and textures, they can articulate what might otherwise remain unsaid, connecting with others in profound and moving ways.

Consider the story of Alex, a young autistic painter whose vibrant landscapes reveal more than just skill; they showcase his emotional depth, his perception of the world, and his unspoken dreams. Before discovering painting, Alex struggled to express his feelings and connect with those around him. Art became his voice, a medium through which he could share his unique view of the world, leading to a newfound sense of belonging and understanding from his community.

Engaging in art not only facilitates emotional expression but also supports cognitive development, enhancing skills such as problem-solving, planning, and fine motor coordination. The process of creating art is therapeutic, providing a sense of calm and focus in a world that can often feel overwhelming. For autistic individuals, the arts are not just hobbies; they are essential channels for communication, self-discovery, and connection. Through art, they tell their stories, share their emotions, and engage with the world on their own terms.

Music as a Universal Language

Music transcends words, reaching into the depths of the soul to express what cannot be spoken. For many on the autism spectrum, it becomes a universal language — one that connects them to their own emotions and to the people around them in a deeply meaningful way. Whether through playing an instrument or simply listening, music offers a unique outlet for self-expression and a bridge to interpersonal connection.

Take, for instance, the experience of Emma, an autistic individual who found her voice through the strings of a violin. Before discovering music, Emma felt isolated, struggling to communicate her emotions and thoughts. The violin became her medium of expression, allowing her to convey her feelings and connect with others on an emotional level that words had never allowed. Through her performances, Emma not only shares her own emotions but also evokes feelings in those who listen, creating a powerful, empathetic bond.

Music therapy has emerged as a beneficial tool in supporting autistic individuals, leveraging the innate power of music to improve communication, social skills, and emotional well-being. The structured yet flexible nature of music therapy sessions provides a safe space for exploration and expression, catering to the individual's needs and preferences. By engaging with music, individuals on the spectrum can experience a sense of achievement, improve their mood, and find joy in the shared human experience of melody and rhythm. Music, with its universal appeal, becomes a key to unlocking potential, fostering connections, and celebrating the unique contributions of each individual.

Exploring Additional Avenues

Beyond the familiar realms of art and music lies a rich landscape of creative expression waiting to be explored. From the rhythmic storytelling of dance to the boundless worlds crafted in writing and the innovative vistas of digital arts, each avenue offers unique opportunities for self-discovery and expression. These forms of creativity are not just activities; they are pathways to understanding and articulating the self in ways words alone cannot achieve.

Consider the magic of dance, where movements become words and emotions are conveyed through the poetry of motion. Daniel, who found traditional communication challenging, discovered in dance a powerful medium to express his joy, frustrations, and dreams. Similarly, in writing, individuals like Sarah find solace and strength, crafting stories and poems that offer glimpses into their inner worlds, connecting with readers on a deeply personal level.

The digital realm opens up new possibilities for creativity, from graphic design and animation to video game development, offering a canvas as limitless as one's imagination. For those like Alex, who revel in the precision and possibility of digital creation, technology becomes a tool of empowerment, enabling them to share their perspectives and innovate within a space where they feel competent and confident.

These creative outlets underscore the inclusive nature of self-expression, accessible to all regardless of ability or interest. By encouraging exploration across these diverse forms of creativity, we invite individuals on the autism spectrum to uncover and share their unique talents and perspectives, fostering a world that celebrates diversity in expression and connection.

Therapeutic Outlets and Their Impact

Creative activities stand as more than mere pastimes; they embody powerful therapeutic outlets, offering profound mental, emotional, and physical benefits. Engaging in creativity is akin to opening a valve that releases the pressures of daily life, allowing individuals to find peace, clarity, and joy in the act of creation. This chapter delves into the holistic impact of these activities, revealing how they serve not just as forms of expression but as essential components of well-being.

The transformative power of creativity can be seen in its ability to soothe the mind, heal the heart, and energize the body. Whether it's the gentle brushstrokes on a canvas, the rhythmic strumming of a guitar, or the fluid movements of a dance, each act of creativity is a step toward inner harmony and balance. This section aims to inspire readers by highlighting the multifaceted benefits of creative outlets, emphasizing their role in fostering a healthier, happier, and more fulfilled life. Let us explore how these activities when embraced fully, can become powerful tools for therapy and transformation.

Art Therapy: Healing Through Creation

Art therapy emerges as a beacon of hope, offering a unique and profound way for autistic individuals to navigate their emotions and experiences. At its core, art therapy provides a non-verbal mode of expression, a sanctuary where words are unnecessary, and feelings and thoughts can take shape in visual form. This therapeutic approach is rooted in the belief that the process of creation can be healing, allowing individuals to explore their inner landscape in a safe and supportive environment.

Art therapy sessions are custom-tailored to meet each person's specific needs and preferences. They become a journey of self-discovery and emotional exploration. Therapists skilled in this modality guide participants through various artistic mediums, helping them find the ones that resonate most deeply with their personal expression and healing process.

Success stories abound, illuminating the transformative impact of art therapy. Take, for example, the case of Lily, a young girl who found herself overwhelmed by the sensory and social demands of her environment. Through art therapy, Lily was able to communicate her anxieties and joys, using colors and shapes to express what she found difficult to say out loud. Over time, her artwork became a bridge to understanding herself and connecting with others, showcasing the profound effect that healing through creation can have.

Art therapy stands not just as a method for coping but as a testament to the strength and resilience of the human spirit. It reaffirms the power of artistic expression as a catalyst for emotional release, personal growth, and, ultimately, healing.

Music Therapy: Harmonizing Emotions

Music therapy operates on the premise that melodies and rhythms can reach us where words cannot, offering a unique pathway to harmonizing our emotions. This therapeutic approach leverages the universal language of music to facilitate communication, emotional regulation, and social interaction, especially for autistic individuals who may find traditional forms of expression challenging. Within the framework of music therapy, the fusion of sounds and silence becomes a powerful tool for connection and understanding.

In music therapy sessions, participants engage in a variety of activities, including playing instruments, singing, listening to music, and even composing their own pieces. These activities are not just about making music; they're about using music as a medium to explore feelings, manage stress, enhance concentration, and build relationships. Therapists tailor these sessions to the individual's needs, creating a supportive environment where participants can express themselves freely and safely.

Evidence of music therapy's positive outcomes is both widespread and deeply moving. Consider the story of Marcus, an autistic teenager who struggled with verbal communication and social anxiety. Through music therapy, he found a way to express his emotions and connect with others, gradually improving his ability to interact and communicate. Marcus's journey is just one of many that highlight how music therapy can provide a harmonious bridge to emotional expression and social engagement, offering a glimpse into the profound impact that music can have on our lives.

The Benefits of Movement: Dance and Physical Expression

Dance and physical forms of creativity, such as theater and martial arts, stand as dynamic gateways to self-expression, emotional release, and physical health. These activities do more than just move the body; they stir the soul, enabling individuals, especially those on the autism spectrum, to communicate in ways words cannot capture. Through the fluidity of movement and the rhythm of dance, individuals find a unique voice, one that speaks in leaps, turns, and the silent language of motion.

The therapeutic benefits of these physical expressions are manifold, encompassing improved motor skills, enhanced coordination, and a deeper connection to one's emotions. Engaging in dance, for instance, offers a structured yet liberating environment where individuals can explore and express feelings while simultaneously developing physical agility and strength. Theater activities, on the other hand, provide a platform for storytelling and role-play, which can boost social skills and self-confidence. Martial arts focus on discipline, focus, and respect for oneself and others, promoting a sense of inner calm and self-control.

Anecdotes from the lives of individuals who have embraced these activities tell a story of transformation. Take Jamie, for example, whose journey into dance therapy unlocked a newfound joy and a way to express his emotions without fear or reservation. Jamie's story, along with countless others, underscores the powerful impact that movement and physical expression can have on well-being, offering a pathway to not just physical health but emotional and social flourishing as well.

Celebrating Achievements Big and Small

Every milestone—no matter its size—deserves recognition and celebration in the journey of creative expression. This act of acknowledgment isn't just about the outcome; it's about honoring the courage, effort, and growth that come with each creative endeavor. Celebrating achievements, both big and small, play a crucial role in boosting confidence, nurturing self-esteem, and fostering a sense of accomplishment. It's a testament to the individual's journey, a reflection of their persistence and resilience.

The beauty of creativity lies not in the perfection of the final product but in the process itself — the moments of inspiration, the challenges overcome, and the joy of expression. By adopting an inclusive approach to celebrating creativity, we send a powerful message: every effort is valuable, every step forward is worth acknowledgment. This chapter prepares you to be inspired by uplifting stories and examples of how individuals on the autism spectrum have found their voice, made their mark, and experienced the joy of creative achievements. Through these narratives, we'll explore the myriad ways achievements can be celebrated, reminding us that in the realm of creativity, every success, no matter how seemingly small, is a cause for celebration.

Showcases and Exhibitions

The act of showcasing creative work in art shows, music performances, or through digital portfolios is a powerful form of validation that transcends the personal realm, connecting creators with a wider community. This public display of creativity is not just an exhibition of talent; it's an invitation into the artist's world, offering a glimpse into their thoughts, emotions, and perspective. The acknowledgment and appreciation from an audience create a positive feedback loop, bolstering the creator's confidence and sense of belonging.

Consider the story of Mia, an autistic artist whose vibrant paintings were first displayed at a local community art show. Initially hesitant to share her work, Mia found the experience transformative. The positive reception not only validated her artistic expression but also connected her with fellow artists and enthusiasts who saw the world through a similar kaleidoscope of colors and shapes. This connection spurred a newfound confidence in Mia, encouraging her to continue exploring and sharing her art.

Similarly, the tale of The Harmonics, a music group comprising autistic individuals, illustrates the power of performance. Their first live concert was met with applause and cheers that echoed far beyond the stage, affirming their musical talents and fostering a sense of achievement and unity among the group members.

These examples underscore the significant role that showcases and exhibitions play in validating creative efforts, building community connections, and reinforcing the importance of every voice in the tapestry of human expression.

Personal Milestones in Creative Expression

In the realm of creativity, every step forward marks a significant milestone in the journey of personal growth and expression. These milestones, whether they are completing a first painting, mastering a new dance move, or writing an original story, embody the essence of progress and the pure joy of creating. Celebrating these achievements acknowledges not just the outcome but the journey itself — the learning, the challenges overcome, and the personal development that occurs along the way.

One such narrative is that of Jonah, who set out to write a short story. What began as a few sentences soon blossomed into pages filled with imaginative worlds and characters. For Jonah, the real achievement was not the completion of the story but the process of writing itself. Each paragraph penned was a step out of his comfort zone, a testament to his growing confidence and ability to articulate his thoughts and dreams.

Similarly, Ella's journey with pottery highlights the significance of personal milestones. Her first successfully thrown pot was more than just a piece of clay; it represented hours of dedication, patience, and self-belief. Ella's joy in this achievement was a reflection of her personal growth, a moment worth celebrating far beyond the confines of the pottery studio.

These stories remind us to cherish and celebrate our creative milestones, no matter how small they may seem. Each step forward is a reflection of personal growth, a cause for joy, and a milestone in the beautiful journey of creative expression.

Encouraging a Culture of Appreciation

Cultivating an environment where every brushstroke, note, and movement is acknowledged and celebrated can transform not just individuals but entire communities. This culture of appreciation for creative expressions, especially from autistic individuals, fosters an atmosphere of inclusion, understanding, and mutual respect. It's about creating spaces — be they in families, schools, or wider community circles — where everyone's creative journey is valued and their achievements, big or small, are recognized.

For parents, this might mean setting up a mini gallery at home to display their child's artwork or organizing family recitals where musical talents can be shared. Educators can dedicate time for students to showcase their creative projects to the class, turning classrooms into forums of diverse expression and appreciation. Communities can host inclusive art fairs or talent shows, providing platforms for autistic individuals to share their gifts with a wider audience.

Such acts of recognition not only boost the confidence of the creators but also educate and enrich the observers, paving the way for a deeper appreciation of diversity and the unique ways people see and interpret the world around them. This culture of appreciation sends a powerful message: that every individual has something valuable to contribute, and their efforts deserve recognition. By fostering this environment, we not only celebrate the achievements of autistic individuals but also contribute to a more inclusive, understanding, and compassionate society.

CONCLUSION

As you turn the final pages, you stand at the precipice of transformation. I hope this book has illuminated the path through the intricate maze of autism, shining a light on both its challenges and its profound beauties. At its essence, our journey together champions empowerment — forged from the deep understanding, unwavering support, and unconditional acceptance of your child's unique worldview.

This book has aimed to equip you with the knowledge, strategies, and emotional tools needed to navigate the challenges and celebrate the victories that come with parenting an autistic child. By embracing your child's individuality, fostering open communication, and creating an environment conducive to their growth, you not only enhance their life but also enrich your own. The journey of understanding autism is ongoing, but with each step, you become more than a parent; you become an advocate, a teacher, and a student of the incredible world your child shares with you.

Throughout this book, we've delved deep into the essence of empathy, the power of communication, the significance of crafting a supportive environment, and the imperative of advocating for neurodiversity. Each chapter was meticulously designed to not only enlighten you about the autistic spectrum but also to arm you with practical strategies that bridge gaps and build connections. Empathy, the first cornerstone, allows you to see the world through your child's eyes, fostering a bond that goes beyond words.

Communication, both verbal and non-verbal, has been demystified, offering you tools to understand and interact with your child in ways that respect their unique processing of the world.

Creating a supportive environment is about more than just physical space; it's about constructing a world where your child feels safe, understood, and free to be themselves. This includes everything from sensory-friendly home adjustments to educating those around you about the importance of acceptance and inclusion. Finally, advocating for neurodiversity is not just a call to action; it's a movement toward a future where every individual is valued for their unique contributions to society. These key takeaways are not merely lessons; they are pillars upon which a nurturing and positive relationship can be built between you, your child, and the world at large. Embracing these principles paves the way for a society that celebrates diversity, encourages inclusion, and fosters understanding and respect for all.

Now, as you stand at the threshold of this journey, I encourage you to take that first, perhaps daunting, step. Embrace the lessons nestled within these pages and begin to apply them to your life. Remember, the path to growth, understanding, and empowerment, though challenging, is immensely rewarding. This book is designed not just as a one-time guide but as a companion for your journey. As you and your child navigate the complexities and joys of autism, let it serve as a beacon of hope, a source of comfort, and a wellspring of strategies.

I invite you to revisit its chapters whenever you need reassurance or seek new insights. Each story, each piece of advice, is a reminder that you are not alone on this path. The journey of understanding and supporting your autistic child is one of profound transformation — not only for them but for you as well. Let this book be your guide, your inspiration, and your support as you move forward, step by step, into a future filled with possibilities. Start today, for the journey of a thousand miles begins with a single step. Together, let's celebrate each milestone, each moment of connection, and every step toward a world that embraces and celebrates neurodiversity.

As we reach the end of this shared journey, I warmly invite you to share your thoughts and experiences with this book through a review. Your feedback is not just invaluable to me as the author, but it serves as a guiding light for other families navigating the complexities of autism. Each review has the power to inspire, comfort, and empower others by spreading a message of hope, understanding, and resilience. By sharing your story, you contribute to a larger narrative of acceptance and celebration of neurodiversity. Let's join hands in building a community that uplifts and supports each other. Your voice can make a difference, encouraging others to embrace the journey with confidence and optimism. Please take a moment to share your review and help spread the word about the transformative power of empathy, understanding, and love.

Printed in Great Britain
by Amazon